THE WORKS OF
EUGENE FIELD

Vol. IX

"Out yonder in the moonlight, wherein God's-acre lies."

Drawn by W. Hamilton Gibson

"Out yonder in the moonlight, wherein God's-acre lies"

Drawn by W. Hamilton Gibson

THE WRITINGS IN PROSE AND VERSE OF EUGENE FIELD

Songs ❧ ❧ AND OTHER VERSE

CHARLES SCRIBNER'S SONS ❧ NEW YORK ❧ 1896

INTRODUCTION

"IT is about impossible for a man to get rid of his Puritan grandfathers, and nobody who has ever had one has ever escaped his Puritan grandmother;" so said Eugene Field to me one sweet April day, when we talked together of the things of the spirit. It is one of his own confessions that he was fond of clergymen. Most preachers are supposed to be helplessly tied up with such a set of limitations that there are but a few jokes which they may tolerate, and a small number of delights into which they may enter. Doubtless many a cheerful soul likes to meet such of the clergy, in order that the worldling may feel the contrast of liberty with bondage, and demonstrate by bombardment of wit and humor, how intellectually thin are the walls against which certain forms of skepticism and fun offend. Eugene Field did not belong to these. He called them "a tribe which do unseemly beset the saints." Nobody has ever had a more numerous or loving clientage of friendship among the ministers of this city than the author of "The Holy Cross" and "The Little Yaller Baby." Those of this number who were closest to the full-hearted singer know that beneath and within all his exquisite wit and ludicrous raillery — so often directed against the shallow formalist, or the unctuous hypocrite — there were an aspiration toward the divine, and a desire for what is often slightingly called "religious conversation," as sincere as it was resistless within him. My own first remembrance of him brings back a conversation which ended in a prayer, and the last sight I had of him was when he said, only four days before his death, "Well, then, we will set the day soon and you will come out and baptize the children."

Some of the most humorous of his letters which have come under the observation of his clerical friends, were addressed to the secretary of one of them. Some little business matters with regard to his readings and the like had acquainted him with a better kind of handwriting than he had been accustomed to receive from his pastor, and, noting the finely appended signature, "per ——— ———," Field wrote a most effusively complimentary letter to his ministerial friend, congratulating him upon the fact that emanations from his office, or parochial study, were "now readable as far West as Buena Park." At length, nothing having appeared in writing by which he might discover that ——— ——— was a lady of his own acquaintance, she whose valuable services he desired to recognize was made the recipient of a series of beautifully illuminated and daintily written letters, all of them quaintly begun, continued, and ended in ecclesiastical terminology, most of them having to do with affairs in which the two gentlemen only were primarily interested, the larger number of them addressed in English to "Brother ———," in care of the minister, and yet others directed in Latin:

INTRODUCTION

Ad Fratrem —— ——
  In curam, Sanctissimi patris ——, doctoris
    divinitatis,
    Apud Institutionem Armouriensem,
      CHICAGO,
        ILLINOIS.

{ Ab Eugenio Agro, }
{   peccatore misere }

Even the mail-carrier appeared to know
what fragrant humor escaped from the en-
velope.

Here is a specimen inclosure:

BROTHER —— : I am to read some of my things before the senior class of the Chicago University next Monday evening. As there is undoubtedly more or less
jealousy between the presidents of the two south side
institutions of learning, I take it upon myself to invite
the lord bishop of Armourville, our holy père, to be
present on that occasion in his pontifical robes and fol-
lowed by all the dignitaries of his see, including yourself.
The processional will occur at 8 o'clock sharp, and the
recessional circa 9:30. Pax vobiscum. Salute the holy
Father with a kiss, and believe me, dear brother,
        Your fellow lamb in the old Adam,
              EUGENIO AGRO.

The First Wednesday after Pay day,
    September 11, 1895.

On an occasion of this lady's visit to the South-west, where Field's fancied association of cowboys and miners was formed, she was fortunate enough to obtain for the decoration of his library the rather extraordinary Indian blanket which often appears in the sketches of his loved workshop, and for the decoration of himself a very fine necktie made of the skin of a diamond-back rattlesnake. Some other friend had given his boys a "vociferant burro." After the presentation was made, though for two years he had met her socially and at the pastor's office, he wrote to the secretary, in acknowledgment, as follows:

DEAR BROTHER ———: I thank you most heartily for the handsome specimens of heathen manufacture which you brought with you for me out of the land of Nod. Mrs. Field is quite charmed with the blanket, but I think I prefer the necktie; the Old Adam predominates in me, and this pelt of the serpent appeals with peculiar force to my appreciation of the vicious and the sinful. Nearly every morning I don that necktie and go out and twist the supersensitive tail of our intelligent imported burro until the profane beast burthens the air with his ribald protests. I shall ask the holy father — Père ——— — to bring you with him when he comes again to pay a parochial visit to my house. I have a fair and gracious daughter into whose companionship I would fain bring so circumspect and diligent a young man as the holy father represents you to be. Therefore, without fear or trembling accompany that saintly man whensoever he says the word. Thereby you shall further make me your debtor. I send you every assurance of cordial regard, and I beg you to salute the holy father for me with a kiss, and may peace be unto his house and unto all that dwell therein.

Always faithfully yours,
EUGENE FIELD.

CHICAGO, MAY 26, 1892.

He became acquainted with the leading ladies of the Aid Society of the Plymouth Church, and was thoroughly interested in their work. Partly in order to say " Good-bye " before his leaving for California in 1893, and partly, no doubt, that he might continue this humorous correspondence, as he did, he hunted up an old number of Peterson's Magazine, containing a very highly colored and elaborate pattern for knit slippers, such as clergymen received at Christmas thirty years ago, and, inclosing it with utmost care, he forwarded it to the aforesaid " Brother —— " with this note:

DEAR BROTHER ———: It has occurred to me that may-
be the sisters of our congregation will want to make our
dear pastor a handsome present this Christmas; so I in-
close a lovely pattern for slippers, and I shall be glad to
ante up my share of the expense, if the sisters decide to
give our dear pastor this beautiful gift. I should like the
pattern better if it had more red in it, but it will do very
nicely. As I intend to go to California very soon,
you'll have to let me know at once what the assessment
per cap. is, or the rest of the sisters will be compelled
to bear the full burthen of the expense. Brother, I
salute you with an holy kiss, and I rejoice with you,
humbly and meekly and without insolent vaunting,
that some of us are not as other men are.

Your fellow-lamb,

EUGENE FIELD,

BUENA PARK, ILL., DECEMBER 4, 1893.

This was only one phase of the life of this
great-hearted man, as it came close to his
friends in the ministry. Other clergymen
who knew him well will not forget his over-
flowing kindness in times of sickness and
weariness. At least one will not forget the
last day of their meeting and the ardor of
the poet's prayer. Religion, as the Christian
life, was not less sacred to him because he
knew how poorly men achieve the task of
living always at the best level, nor did the

reality of the soul's approach to God grow less noble or commanding to him because he knew that too seldom do we lift our voices heavenward. I am permitted to copy this one letter addressed to a clerical friend, at a time when Eugene Field responded to the call of that undying puritanism in his blood:

DEAR, DEAR FRIEND: I was greatly shocked to read in the *Post* last night of your dangerous illness. It is so seldom that I pray that when I do God knows I am in earnest. I do not pester Him with small matters. It is only when I am in real want that I get down on my wicked knees and pray. And I prayed for you last night, dear friend, for your friendship — the help that it is to me — is what I need, and I cannot be bereft of it. God has always been good to me, and He has said yes to my prayer, I am sure. Others, too — thousands of them — are praying for you, and for your restoration to health; none other has had in it more love and loyalty than my prayer had, and none other, dear friend, among the thousands whom you have blessed with your sweet friendship, loves you better than I do.

EUGENE FIELD.

BUENA PARK, NOVEMBER 15, 1893.

I am still sick abed and I find it hard to think out and write a letter. Read between the lines and the love there will comfort you more than my faulty words can.

I have often thought, as I saw him through his later years espousing the noblest causes with true-hearted zeal, of what he once said in the old "Saints' and Sinners' Corner" when a conversation sprang up on the death of Professor David Swing. His words go far to explain to me that somewhat reckless humor which oftentimes made it seem that he loved to imitate and hold in the pillory of his own inimitable powers of mimicry some of the least attractive forms of the genus *parson* he had seen and known. He said: "A good many things I do and say are things I have to employ to keep down the intention of those who wanted me to be a parson. I guess their desire got into my blood, too, for I have always to preach some little verses or I cannot get through Christmastide."

He had to get on with blood which was exquisitely harmonious with the heart of the Christ. He was not only a born member of the Society for the Prevention of Sorrow to Mankind, but he was by nature a champion of a working Society for the Prevention of Cruelty to Animals. This society was composed of himself. He wished to enlarge the membership of this latter association, but nobody was as orthodox in the faith as to the nobility of a balky horse, and he found none as intolerant of ill-treatment toward any and every brute, as was he. Professor Swing had written and read at the Parliament of Religions an essay on the Humane Treatment of the Brutes, which became a classic before the ink was dry, and one day Field proposed to him and another clergyman that they begin a practical crusade. On those cold days, drivers were demanding impossible things of smooth-shod horses on icy streets, and he saw many a noble beast on his knees, "begging me," as he said, "to get him a priest." Field's scheme was that the delicate and intelligent seer, David Swing, and his less refined and less gentle contemporary should go with him to the City Hall and be sworn in as special policemen and "do up these fellows." His clear blue eye was like a palpitating morning sky, and his whole thin and tall frame shook with passionate missionary zeal. "Ah," said he, as the beloved knight of the unorthodox explained that if he undertook the proposed task he would surely have to abandon all other work, "I never was satisfied that you were orthodox." His other friend had already fallen in his estimate as to fitness for such work. For, had not Eugene Field once started out to pay a bill of fifteen dollars, and had he not met a semblance of a man on the street who was beating a lengthily under-jawed and bad-eyed bull-dog of his own, for some misdemeanor? "Yea, verily," confessed the poet-humorist, who was then a reformer. "Why didn't you have him arrested, Eugene?" "Why, well, I was going jingling along with some new verses in my heart, and I knew I'd lose the *tempo* if I became militant. I said, 'What 'll you take for him?' The pup was so homely that his face ached, but, as I was in a hurry to get to work, I gave him the fifteen dollars, and took the beast to the office." For a solitary remark uttered at the conclusion of this relation and fully confirmed as to its justness by an observation of the dog, his only other human prop for this enterprise was discarded. "Oh, you won't do," he said.

Christianity was increasingly dear to him as the discovery of childhood and the unfolding of its revelations. Into what long disquisitions he delighted to go, estimating the probable value of the idea that all returning to righteousness must be a child's returning. He saw what an influence such a conception has upon the hard and fast lines of habit and destiny to melt them down. He had a still greater estimate of the importance of the fact that Jesus of Nazareth came and lived as a child; and the dream of the last year of his life was to write, in the mood of the Holy-Cross tale, a sketch of the early years of the Little Galilean Peasant-Boy. This vision drifted its light into all his pictures of children at the last. He knew the "Old Adam" in us all, especially as he reappeared in the little folk. "But I don't believe the depravity is total, do you?" he said, "else a child would not care to hear about Mary's Little One;"—and then he would go on, following the Carpenter's Son about the cottage and over the hill, and rejoicing that, in following Him thus, he came back to his own open-eyed childhood.

"But, you know," said he, "my child-hood was full of the absurdities and strenu-osities" (this last was his word) "of my puritan surroundings. Why, I never knew how naturally and easily I can get back into the veins of an old puritan grandfather that one of my grandmothers must have had — and how hard it is for me to behave there, until I read Alice Morse Earle's 'The Sab-bath in New England.' I read that book nearly all night, if haply I might subdue the confusion and sorrows that were wrought in me by eating a Christmas pie on that feast-day. The fact is, my immediate eccle-siastical belongings are Episcopalian. I am of the church of Archbishop Laud and King Charles of blessed memory. I like good, thick Christmas pie, 'reeking with sapid juices,' full-ripe and zealous for good or ill. But my 'Separatist' ancestors all mistook gastric difficulties for spiritual graces, and, living in me, they all revolt and want to sail in the Mayflower, or hold town-meetings inside of me after feast-day."

Then, as if he had it in his mind, — poor, pale, yellow-skinned sufferer, — to attract

one to the book he delighted in, he related
that he fell asleep with this delicious volume
in his hand, and this is part of the dream he
sketched afterward;

"I went alone to the meeting-house the
which those who are sinfully inclined toward
Rome would call a ' church,' and it was on
the Sabbath day. I yearned and strove to
repent me of the merry mood and full sorry
humors of Christmastide. For did not Judge
Sewall make public his confession of having
an overwhelming sense of inward condem-
nation for having opposed the Almighty
with the witches of Salem ? I fancied that
one William F. Poole of the Newberry
Library went also to comfort me and
strengthen, as he would fain have done for
the Judge. Not one of us carried a cricket,
though Friend Poole related that he had left
behind a ' seemly brassen foot-stove ' full of
hot coals from his hearthstone. On the day
before, Pelitiah Underwood, the wolf-killer,
had destroyed a fierce beast; and now the
head thereof was ' nayled to the meeting-
house with a notice thereof.' It grinned at
me and spit forth fire such as I felt within

me. I was glad to enter the house, which was 'lathed on the inside and so daubed and whitened over workmanlike.' I had not been there, as it bethought me, since the day of the raising, when Jonathan Strong did 'break his thy,' and when all made complaint that only £9 had been spent for liquor, punch, beere, and flip, for the raising, whereas, on the day of the ordination, even at supper-time, besides puddings of corn meal and 'sewet baked therein, pyes, tarts, beare-stake and deer-meat,' there were 'cyder, rum-bitters, sling, old Barbadoes spirit, and Josslyn's nectar, made of Maligo raisins, spices, and syrup of clove gilly-flowers'— all these given out freely to the worshippers over a newly made bar at the church door — God be praised! As I mused on this merry ordination, the sounding-board above the pulpit appeared as if to fall upon the pulpit, whereon I read, after much effort: '*Holiness is the Lord's.*' The tassels and carved pomegranates on the sounding-board became living creatures and changed themselves into grimaces, and I was woefully wrought upon by the red cushion on the pulpit, which did seem a bag of fire. As the minister was heard coming up the winding stairs unseen, and, yet more truly, as his head at length appeared through the open trap-doorway, I thought him Satan, and, but for friend Poole, I had cried out lustily in fear. Terror fled me when I considered that none might do any harm there. For was not the church militant now assembled? Besides, had they not obeyed the law of the General Court that each congregation should carry a ' competent number of pieces, fixed and complete with powder and shot and swords, every Lord's-day at the meeting-house ?' And, right well equipped ' with psalm-book, shot and powder-horn' sat that doughty man, Shear Yashub Millard along with Hezekiah Bristol and four others whose issue I have known pleasantly in the flesh here; and those of us who had no pieces wore ' coats basted with cotton-wool, and thus made defensive against Indian arrows.' Yet it bethought me that there was no defence against what I had devoured on Christmas day. I had rather been the least of these,— even he who 'blew the Kunk' — than to be thus seated there and afeared that the brethren in the 'pitts' doubted I had true religion. That I had found a proper seat — even this I wot not; and I quaked, for had not two of my kin been fined near unto poverty for 'disorderly going and setting in seats not theirs by any means,' so great was their sin. It had not yet come upon the day when there was a 'dignifying of the meeting.' Did not even the pious Judge Sewall's second spouse once sit in the foreseat when he thought to have taken her into 'his own pue?' and, she having died in a few months, did not that godly man exclaim: 'God in his holy Sovereignity put my wife out of the Foreseat'? Was I not also in recollection by many as one who once 'prophaned the Lord's Day in ye meeting-house, in ye times of ye forenoone service, by my rude and Indecent acting in Laughing and other Doings by my face with Tabatha Morgus, against ye peace of our Sovereign Lord ye King, His crown and Dignity?'

At this, it appears that I groaned in my sleep, for I was not only asleep here and now, but I was dreaming that I was asleep there and then, in the meeting-house. It was in this latter sleep that I groaned so heavily in spirit and in body that the tithing-man, or awakener, did approach me from behind, without stopping to brush me to awakening by the fox-taile which was fixed to the end of his long staffe, or even without painfully sticking into my body his sharp and pricking staffe which he did sometimes use. He led me out bodily to the noone-house, where I found myself fully awakened, but much broken in spirit. Then and there did I write these verses, which I send to you:

" Mother," says I, " is that a pie?" in tones akin to
  scorning ;
" It is, my son," quoth she, " and one full ripe for
  Christmas morning !
It 's fat with plums as big as your thumbs, reeking with
  sapid juices,
And you 'll find within all kinds of sin our grocery
  store produces ! "
       " O, well," says I,
       "Seein' it 's *pie*
    And is guaranteed to please, ma'am,
       By your advice,
       I 'll take a slice,
  If you 'll kindly pass the cheese, ma'am ! "

But once a year comes Christmas cheer, and one should
  then be merry,
But as for me, as you can see, I 'm disconcerted, very;
For that pesky pie sticks grimly by my organs of diges-
  tion,
And that 't will stay by me till May or June I make no
  question.
    So unto you,
    ·Good friends and true,
  I 'll tip this solemn warning:
    At every price,
    Eschew the vice
  ·Of eating pie in the morning.

      FRANK W. GUNSAULUS.
CHICAGO, March, 1896.

The Contents of this Book

CONTENTS

xxvi

CONTENTS

❦

Songs and Other Verse

❦

THE SINGING IN GOD'S ACRE

UT yonder in the moonlight, where-
    in God's Acre lies,
    Go angels walking to and fro, sing-
ing their lullabies.
Their radiant wings are folded, and their eyes
    are bended low,
As they sing among the beds whereon the
    flowers delight to grow,—

      " Sleep, oh, sleep!
      The Shepherd guardeth His sheep.
Fast speedeth the night away,
Soon cometh the glorious day;
Sleep, weary ones, while ye may,
      Sleep, oh, sleep ! "

The flowers within God's Acre see that fair
and wondrous sight,
And hear the angels singing to the sleepers
through the night;
And, lo! throughout the hours of day those
gentle flowers prolong
The music of the angels in that tender
slumber-song,—

"Sleep, oh, sleep!
The Shepherd loveth His sheep.
He that guardeth His flock the best
Hath folded them to His loving breast;
So sleep ye now, and take your rest,—
Sleep, oh, sleep!"

From angel and from flower the years have
learned that soothing song,
And with its heavenly music speed the days
and nights along;
So through all time, whose flight the Shepherd's vigils glorify,
God's Acre slumbereth in the grace of that
sweet lullaby,—

4

"Sleep, oh, sleep!
The Shepherd loveth His sheep.
Fast speedeth the night away,
Soon cometh the glorious day;
Sleep, weary ones, while ye may,—
Sleep, oh, sleep!"

THE DREAM-SHIP

WHEN the world is fast asleep,
    Along the midnight skies —
As though it were a wandering cloud —
    The ghostly dream-ship flies.

An angel stands at the dream-ship's helm,
    An angel stands at the prow,
And an angel stands at the dream-ship's side
    With a rue-wreath on her brow.

The other angels, silver-crowned,
    Pilot and helmsman are,
And the angel with the wreath of rue
    Tosseth the dreams afar.

The dreams they fall on rich and poor;
    They fall on young and old;
And some are dreams of poverty,
    And some are dreams of gold.

And some are dreams that thrill with joy,
    And some that melt to tears;
Some are dreams of the dawn of love,
    And some of the old dead years.

On rich and poor alike they fall,
    Alike on young and old,
Bringing to slumbering earth their joys
    And sorrows manifold.

The friendless youth in them shall do
    The deeds of mighty men,
And drooping age shall feel the grace
    Of buoyant youth again.

The king shall be a beggarman —
    The pauper be a king —
In that revenge or recompense
    The dream-ship dreams do bring.

So ever downward float the dreams
    That are for all and me,
And there is never mortal man
    Can solve that mystery.

7

But ever onward in its course
    Along the haunted skies —
As though it were a cloud astray —
    The ghostly dream-ship flies.

Two angels with their silver crowns
    Pilot and helmsman are,
And an angel with a wreath of rue
    Tosseth the dreams afar.

TO CINNA

CINNA, the great Venusian told
    In songs that will not die
How in Augustan days of old
    Your love did glorify
His life and all his being seemed
    Thrilled by that rare incense
Till, grudging him the dreams he dreamed,
    The gods did call you hence.

Cinna, I 've looked into your eyes,
    And held your hands in mine,
And seen your cheeks in sweet surprise
    Blush red as Massic wine;
Now let the songs in Cinna's praise
    Be chanted once again,
For, oh! alone I walk the ways
    We walked together then!

9

Perhaps upon some star to-night,
　　So far away in space
I cannot see that beacon light
　　Nor feel its soothing grace —
Perhaps from that far-distant sphere
　　Her quickened vision seeks
For this poor heart of mine that here
　　To its lost Cinna speaks.

Then search this heart, beloved eyes,
　　And find it still as true
As when in all my boyhood skies
　　My guiding stars were you!
Cinna, you know the mystery
　　That is denied to men —
Mine is the lot to feel that we
　　Shall elsewhere love again!

BALLAD OF WOMEN I LOVE

PRUDENCE MEARS hath an old blue
   plate
   Hid away in an oaken chest,
And a Franklin platter of ancient date
   Beareth Amandy Baker's crest;
What times soever I 've been their guest,
   Says I to myself in an undertone:
" Of womenfolk, it must be confessed,
   These do I love, and these alone."

Well, again, in the Nutmeg State,
   Dorothy Pratt is richly blest
With a relic of art and a land effete —
   A pitcher of glass that 's cut, not pressed.
And a Washington teapot is possessed
   Down in Pelham by Marthy Stone—
Think ye now that I say in jest
   " These do I love, and these alone ? "

Were Hepsy Higgins inclined to mate,
    Or Dorcas Eastman prone to invest
In Cupid's bonds, they could find their fate
    In the bootless bard of Crockery Quest.
For they 've heaps of trumpery — so have the
    rest
    Of those spinsters whose ware I 'd like
    to own;
You can see why I say with such certain zest,
    " These do I love, and these alone."

ENVOY

Prince, show me the quickest way and best
    To gain the subject of my moan;
We 've neither spinsters nor relics out West —
    These do I love, and these alone.

SUPPOSE

SUPPOSE, my dear, that you were I
    And by your side your sweetheart sate;
Suppose you noticed by and by
    The distance 'twixt you were too great;
Now tell me, dear, what would you do?
    I know — and so do you.

And when (so comfortably placed)
    Suppose you only grew aware
That that dear, dainty little waist
    Of hers looked very lonely there;
Pray tell me sooth — what would you do?
    I know, and so do you.

When, having done what I just did
    With not a frown to check or chill,
Suppose her red lips seemed to bid
    Defiance to your lordly will;
Oh, tell me, sweet, what would you do?
    I know, and so do you.

MYSTERIOUS DOINGS

AS once I rambled in the woods
   I chanced to spy amid the brake
A huntsman ride his way beside
   A fair and passing tranquil lake;
Though velvet bucks sped here and there,
   He let them scamper through the green—
Not one smote he, but lustily
   He blew his horn—what could it mean?

As on I strolled beside that lake,
   A pretty maid I chanced to see
Fishing away for finny prey,
   Yet not a single one caught she;
All round her boat the fishes leapt
   And gambolled to their hearts' content,
Yet never a thing did the maid but sing—
   I wonder what on earth it meant.

14

As later yet I roamed my way,
  A lovely steed neighed loud and long,
And an empty boat sped all afloat
  Where sang a fishermaid her song;
All underneath the prudent shade,
  Which yonder kindly willows threw,
Together strayed a youth and maid —
  I can't explain it all, can you?

WITH TWO SPOONS FOR TWO SPOONS

HOW trifling shall these gifts appear
  Among the splendid many
That loving friends now send to cheer
  Harvey and Ellen Jenney.

And yet these baubles symbolize
  A certain fond relation
That well beseems, as I surmise,
  This festive celebration.

Sweet friends of mine, be spoons once more,
  And with your tender cooing
Renew the keen delights of yore —
  The rapturous bliss of wooing.

16

What though that silver in your hair
    Tells of the years aflying?
'T is yours to mock at Time and Care
    With love that is undying.

In memory of this Day, dear friends,
    Accept the modest token
From one who with the bauble sends
    A love that can't be spoken.

MARY SMITH

AWAY down East where I was reared
amongst my Yankee kith,
There used to live a pretty girl whose name
was Mary Smith;
And though it 's many years since last I saw
that pretty girl,
And though I feel I 'm sadly worn by West-
ern strife and whirl;
Still, oftentimes, I think about the old famil-
iar place,
Which, someway, seemed the brighter for
Miss Mary's pretty face,
And in my heart I feel once more revivified
the glow
I used to feel in those old times when I was
Mary's beau.

I saw her home from singing school — she
    warbled like a bird.
A sweeter voice than hers for song or speech
    I never heard.
She was soprano in the choir, and I a solemn
    bass,
And when we unisoned our voices filled that
    holy place;
The tenor and the alto never had the slight-
    est chance,
For Mary's upper register made every heart-
    string dance;
And, as for me, I shall not brag, and yet I 'd
    have you know
I sung a very likely bass when I was Mary's
    beau.

On Friday nights I 'd drop around to make
    my weekly call,
And though I came to visit her, I 'd have to
    see 'em all.
With Mary's mother sitting here and Mary's
    father there,
The conversation never flagged so far as I 'm
    aware;

Sometimes I'd hold her worsted, sometimes
    we'd play at games,
Sometimes dissect the apples which we'd
    named each other's names.
Oh how I loathed the shrill-toned clock that
    told me when to go —
'T was ten o'clock at half-past eight when
    I was Mary's beau.

Now there was Luther Baker — because he'd
    come of age
And thought himself some pumpkins be-
    cause he drove the stage —
He fancied he could cut me out; but Mary
    was my friend —
Elsewise I'm sure the issue had had a tragic
    end.
For Luther Baker was a man I never could
    abide,
And, when it came to Mary, either he or I
    had died.
I merely cite this instance incidentally to
    show
That I was quite in earnest when I was
    Mary's beau.

20

How often now those sights, those pleasant
    sights, recur again:
The little township that was all the world
    I knew of then —
The meeting-house upon the hill, the tavern
    just beyond,
Old deacon Packard's general store, the saw-
    mill by the pond,
The village elms I vainly sought to conquer
    in my quest
Of that surpassing trophy, the golden oriole's
    nest.
And, last of all those visions that come back
    from long ago,
The pretty face that thrilled my soul when I
    was Mary's beau.

Hush, gentle wife, there is no need a pang
    should vex your heart —
'T is many years since fate ordained that she
    and I should part;
To each a true, maturer love came in good
    time, and yet
It brought not with its nobler grace the
    power to forget.

21

And would you fain begrudge me now the
    sentimental joy
That comes of recollections of my sparkings
    when a boy ?
I warrant me that, were your heart put to
    the rack, 't would show
That it had predilections when I was Mary's
    beau.

And, Mary, should these lines of mine seek
    out your biding place,
God grant they bring the old sweet smile
    back to your pretty face —
God grant they bring you thoughts of me,
    not as I am to-day,
With faltering step and brimming eyes and
    aspect grimly gray;
But thoughts that picture me as fair and full
    of life and glee
As *we* were in the olden times — as *you*
    shall always be.
Think of me ever, Mary, as the boy you used
    to know
When time was fleet, and life was sweet,
    and I was Mary's beau.

Dear hills of old New England, look down
    with tender eyes
Upon one little lonely grave that in your
    bosom lies;
For in that cradle sleeps a child who was so
    fair to see
God yearned to have unto Himself the joy
    she brought to me;
And bid your winds sing soft and low the
    song of other days,
When, hand in hand and heart to heart, we
    went our pleasant ways —
Ah me! but could I sing again that song of
    long ago,
Instead of this poor idle song of being Mary's
    beau.

JESSIE

WHEN I remark her golden hair
    Swoon on her glorious shoulders,
I marvel not that sight so rare
    Doth ravish all beholders;
For summon hence all pretty girls
    Renowned for beauteous tresses,
And you shall find among their curls
    There 's none so fair as Jessie's.

And Jessie's eyes are, oh, so blue
    And full of sweet revealings —
They seem to look you through and through
    And read your inmost feelings;
Nor black emits such ardent fires,
    Nor brown such truth expresses —
Admit it, all ye gallant squires —
    There are no eyes like Jessie's.

24

Her voice (like liquid beams that roll
    From moonland to the river)
Steals subtly to the raptured soul,
    Therein to lie and quiver;
Or falls upon the grateful ear
    With chaste and warm caresses —
Ah, all concede the truth (who hear):
    There 's no such voice as Jessie's.

Of other charms she hath such store
    All rivalry excelling,
Though I used adjectives galore,
    They 'd fail me in the telling;
But now discretion stays my hand —
    Adieu, eyes, voice, and tresses.
Of all the husbands in the land
    There 's none so fierce as Jessie's.

TO EMMA ABBOTT

THERE — let thy hands be folded
    Awhile in sleep's repose;
The patient hands that wearied not,
But earnestly and nobly wrought
      In charity and faith;
    And let thy dear eyes close —
The eyes that looked alway to God,
Nor quailed beneath the chastening rod
      Of sorrow;
Fold thou thy hands and eyes
      For just a little while,
        And with a smile
          Dream of the morrow.

And, O white voiceless flower,
    The dream which thou shalt dream
Should be a glimpse of heavenly things,
For yonder like a seraph sings
      The sweetness of a life
      With faith alway its theme;

While speedeth from those realms above
The messenger of that dear love
    That healeth sorrow.
  So sleep a little while,
    For thou shalt wake and sing
    Before thy King
      When cometh the morrow.

THE GREAT JOURNALIST IN SPAIN

GOOD editor Dana — God bless him, we
    say —
  Will soon be afloat on the main,
    Will be steaming away
    Through the mist and the spray
  To the sensuous climate of Spain.

Strange sights shall he see in that beautiful
    land
  Which is famed for its soap and its Moor,
    For, as we understand,
    The scenery is grand
  Though the system of railways is poor.

For moonlight of silver and sunlight of gold
  Glint the orchards of lemons and mangoes,
    And the ladies, we 're told,
    Are a joy to behold
  As they twine in their lissome fandangoes.

What though our friend Dana shall twang a
     guitar
  And murmur a passionate strain;
     Oh, fairer by far
     Than those ravishments are
  The castles abounding in Spain.

These castles are built as the builder may
     list —
  They are sometimes of marble or stone,
     But they mostly consist
     Of east wind and mist
  With an ivy of froth overgrown.

A beautiful castle our Dana shall raise
  On a futile foundation of hope,
     And its glories shall blaze
     In the somnolent haze
  Of the mythical lake del y Soap.

The fragrance of sunflowers shall swoon on
     the air
  And the visions of Dreamland obtain,
     And the song of "World's Fair"
     Shall be heard everywhere
  Through that beautiful castle in Spain.

LOVE SONG — HEINE

MANY a beauteous flower doth spring
    From the tears that flood my eyes,
And the nightingale doth sing
    In the burthen of my sighs.

If, O child, thou lovest me,
    Take these flowerets fair and frail,
And my soul shall waft to thee
    Love songs of the nightingale.

THE STODDARDS

WHEN I am in New York, I like to drop
    around at night,
To visit with my honest, genial friends, the
    Stoddards hight;
Their home in Fifteenth street is all so snug,
    and furnished so,
That, when I once get planted there, I don't
    know when to go ;
A cosy cheerful refuge for the weary home-
    sick guest,
Combining Yankee comforts with the free-
    dom of the west.

The first thing you discover, as you maunder
    through the hall,
Is a curious little clock upon a bracket on the
    wall;

'T was made by Stoddard's father, and it 's
    very, very old —
The connoisseurs assure me it is worth its
    weight in gold;
And I, who 've bought all kinds of clocks,
    'twixt Denver and the Rhine,
Cast envious eyes upon that clock, and wish
    that it were mine.

But in the parlor.   Oh, the gems on tables,
    walls, and floor —
Rare first editions, etchings, and old crock-
    ery galore.
Why, talk about the Indies and the wealth
    of Orient things —
They could n't hold a candle to these quaint
    and sumptuous things;
In such profusion, too — Ah me! how dearly
    I recall
How I have sat and watched 'em and wished
    I had 'em all.

Now, Mr. Stoddard's study is on the second
    floor,
A wee blind dog barks at me as I enter
    through the door;

The Cerberus would fain begrudge what
    sights it cannot see,
The rapture of that visual feast it cannot
    share with me;
A miniature edition this — this most absurd
    of hounds —
A genuine unique, I 'm sure, and one un-
    known to Lowndes.

Books — always books — are piled around;
    some musty, and all old;
Tall, solemn folios such as Lamb declared
    he loved to hold;
Large paper copies with their virgin margins
    white and wide,
And presentation volumes with the author's
    comps. inside;
I break the tenth commandment with a wild
    impassioned cry:
Oh, how came Stoddard by these things?
    Why Stoddard, and not I?

From yonder wall looks Thackeray upon his
    poet friend,
And underneath the genial face appear the
    lines he penned;

And here, gadzooks, ben honge ye prynte of
    marvaillous renowne
Yt shameth Chaucers gallaunt knyghtes in
    Canterbury towne;
And still more books and pictures. I 'm
    dazed, bewildered, vexed;
Since I 've broke the tenth commandment,
    why not break the eighth one next?

And, furthermore, in confidence inviolate
    be it said
Friend Stoddard owns a lock of hair that
    grew on Milton's head;
Now I have Gladstone axes and a lot of curi-
    ous things,
Such as pimply Dresden teacups and old
    German wedding-rings;
But nothing like that saintly lock have I on
    wall or shelf,
And, being somewhat short of hair, I should
    like that lock myself.

But Stoddard has a soothing way, as though
    he grieved to see
Invidious torments prey upon a nice young
    chap like me.

34

He waves me to an easy chair and hands me
    out a weed
And pumps me full of that advice he seems
    to know I need;
So sweet the tap of his philosophy and
    knowledge flows
That I can't help wishing that I knew a half
    what Stoddard knows.

And so we sit for hours and hours, praising
    without restraint
The people who are thoroughbreds, and
    roasting the ones that ain't;
Happy, thrice happy, is the man we happen
    to admire,
But wretched, oh, how wretched he that
    hath provoked our ire;
For I speak emphatic English when I once
    get fairly r'iled,
And Stoddard's wrath 's an Ossa upon a
    Pelion piled.

Out yonder, in the alcove, a lady sits and
    darns,
And interjects remarks that always serve to
    spice our yarns;

She's Mrs. Stoddard; there's a dame that's
    truly to my heart:
A tiny little woman, but so quaint, and good,
    and smart
That, if you asked me to suggest which one
    I should prefer
Of all the Stoddard treasures, I should
    promptly mention her.

O dear old man, how I should like to be with
    you this night,
Down in your home in Fifteenth street,
    where all is snug and bright;
Where the shaggy little Cerberus dreams in
    its cushioned place,
And the books and pictures all around smile
    in their old friend's face;
Where the dainty little sweetheart, whom
    you still were proud to woo,
Charms back the tender memories so dear
    to her and you.

THE THREE TAILORS

I SHALL tell you in rhyme how, once on
a time,
Three tailors tramped up to the inn Ingle-
heim,
      On the Rhine, lovely Rhine;
They were broke, but the worst of it all,
they were curst
With that malady common to tailors — a
thirst
      For wine, lots of wine.

"Sweet host," quoth the three, "we 're
hard up as can be,
Yet skilled in the practice of cunning are we,
      On the Rhine, genial Rhine;
And we pledge you we will impart you that
skill
Right quickly and fully, providing you 'll fill
      Us with wine, cooling wine."

But that host shook his head, and he warily
    said:
"Though cunning be good, we take money
    instead,
        On the Rhine, thrifty Rhine;
If ye fancy ye may without pelf have your
    way
You 'll find that there 's both host and the
    devil to pay
        For your wine, costly wine."

Then the first knavish wight took his needle
    so bright
And threaded its eye with a wee ray of light
        From the Rhine, sunny Rhine;
And, in such a deft way, patched a mirror
    that day
That where it was mended no expert could
    say —
        Done so fine 't was for wine.

The second thereat spied a poor little gnat
Go toiling along on his nose broad and flat
        Towards the Rhine, pleasant Rhine;
"Aha, tiny friend, I should hate to offend,

But your stockings need darning" —which
    same did he mend,
        All for wine, soothing wine.

And next there occurred what you 'll deem
    quite absurd —
His needle a space in the wall thrust the third,
        By the Rhine, wondrous Rhine;
And then all so spry, he leapt through the eye
Of that thin cambric needle — nay, think you
    I 'd lie
        About wine — not for wine.

The landlord allowed (with a smile) he was
    proud
To do the fair thing by that talented crowd
        On the Rhine, generous Rhine.
So a thimble filled he as full as could be —
"Drink long and drink hearty, my jolly
    friends three,
        Of my wine, filling wine."

THE JAFFA AND JERUSALEM RAILWAY

A TORTUOUS double iron track; a station here, a station there;
A locomotive, tender, tanks; a coach with
stiff reclining chair;
Some postal cars, and baggage, too; a ves-
tibule of patent make;
With buffers, duffers, switches, and the
soughing automatic brake —
This is the Orient's novel pride, and Syria's
gaudiest modern gem:
The railway scheme that is to ply 'twixt Jaffa
and Jerusalem.

Beware, O sacred Mooley cow, the engine
when you hear its bell;
Beware, O camel, when resounds the whis-
tle's shrill, unholy swell;

And, native of that guileless land, unused to
    modern travel's snare,
Beware the fiend that peddles books — the
    awful peanut-boy beware.
Else, trusting in their specious arts, you may
    have reason to condemn
The traffic which the knavish ply 'twixt
    Jaffa and Jerusalem.

And when, ah, when the bonds fall due,
    how passing wroth will wax the state
From Nebo's mount to Nazareth will spread
    the cry " Repudiate "!
From Hebron to Tiberius, from Jordan's
    banks unto the sea,
Will rise profuse anathemas against
    "that —— monopoly!"
And F. M. B. A. shepherd-folk, with Sock-
    less Jerry leading them,
Will swamp that corporation line 'twixt
    Jaffa and Jerusalem.

HUGO'S "POOL IN THE FOREST"

HOW calm, how beauteous and how
   cool —
   How like a sister to the skies,
Appears the broad, transparent pool
   That in this quiet forest lies.
The sunshine ripples on its face,
   And from the world around, above,
It hath caught down the nameless grace
   Of such reflections as we love.

But deep below its surface crawl
   The reptile horrors of the night —
The dragons, lizards, serpents — all
   The hideous brood that hate the light;
Through poison fern and slimy weed
   And under ragged, jagged stones
They scuttle, or, in ghoulish greed,
   They lap a dead man's bleaching bones.

And as, O pool, thou dost cajole
    With seemings that beguile us well,
So doeth many a human soul
    That teemeth with the lusts of hell.

A RHINE-LAND DRINKING SONG

IF our own life is the life of a flower
  (And that 's what some sages are think-
    ing),
We should moisten the bud with a health-
    giving flood
        And 't will bloom all the sweeter —
        Yes, life 's the completer
    For drinking,
            and drinking,
                    and drinking.

If it be that our life is a journey
    (As many wise folk are opining),
We should sprinkle the way with the rain
    while we may;
        Though dusty and dreary,
        'T is made cool and cheery
    With wining,
            and wining,
                    and wining.

If this life that we live be a dreaming
    (As pessimist people are thinking),
To induce pleasant dreams there is nothing,
    meseems,
        Like this sweet prescription,
        That baffles description —
    This drinking,
           and drinking,
                and drinking.

DER MANN IM KELLER

HOW cool and fair this cellar where
   My throne a dusky cask is;
To do no thing but just to sing
   And drown the time my task is.
         The cooper he 's
         Resolved to please,
And, answering to my winking,
         He fills me up
         Cup after cup
For drinking, drinking, drinking.

         Begrudge me not
         This cosy spot
In which I am reclining —
         Why, who would burst
         With envious thirst,
When he can live by wining.
A roseate hue seems to imbue
   The world on which I 'm blinking;
My fellow-men — I love them when
I 'm drinking, drinking, drinking.

And yet I think, the more I drink,
    It 's more and more I pine for —
Oh, such as I (forever dry)
      God made this land of Rhine for;
        And there is bliss
        In knowing this,
As to the floor I 'm sinking:
      I 've wronged no man
      And never can
While drinking, drinking, drinking.

TWO IDYLLS FROM BION THE SMYRNEAN

I

ONCE a fowler, young and artless,
    To the quiet greenwood came;
Full of skill was he and heartless
    In pursuit of feathered game.
And betimes he chanced to see
Eros perching in a tree.

"What strange bird is that, I wonder?"
    Thought the youth, and spread his snare;
Eros, chuckling at the blunder,
    Gayly scampered here and there.
Do his best, the simple clod
Could not snare the agile god!

Blubbering, to his aged master
    Went the fowler in dismay,
And confided his disaster
    With that curious bird that day;

"Master, hast thou ever heard
Of so ill-disposed a bird?"

"Heard of him?   Aha, most truly!"
    Quoth the master with a smile;
"And thou too, shall know him duly —
    Thou art young, but bide awhile,
And old Eros will not fly
From thy presence by and by!

"For when thou art somewhat older
    That same Eros thou didst see,
More familiar grown and bolder,
    Shall become acquaint with thee;
And when Eros comes thy way
Mark my word, he comes to stay!"

II

Once came Venus to me, bringing
    Eros where my cattle fed —
"Teach this little boy your singing,
    Gentle herdsman," Venus said.
I was young — I did not know
    Whom it was that Venus led —
That was many years ago!

In a lusty voice but mellow —
    Callow pedant! I began
To instruct the little fellow
    In the mysteries known to man;
Sung the noble cithern's praise,
    And the flute of dear old Pan,
And the lyre that Hermes plays.

But he paid no heed unto me —
    Nay, that graceless little boy
Coolly plotted to undo me —
    With his songs of tender joy;
And my pedantry o'erthrown,
    Eager was I to employ
His sweet ritual for mine own!

Ah, these years of ours are fleeting!
    Yet I have not vainly wrought,
Since to-day I am repeating
    What dear lessons Eros taught;
Love, and always love, and then —
    Counting all things else for naught —
Love and always love again!

THE WOOING OF THE SOUTHLAND

(ALASKAN BALLAD)

THE Northland reared his hoary head
    And spied the Southland leagues
        away —
"Fairest of all fair brides," he said,
    "Be thou my bride, I pray!"

Whereat the Southland laughed and cried:
    "I 'll bide beside my native sea,
And I shall never be thy bride
    Till thou com'st wooing me!"

The Northland's heart was a heart of ice,
    A diamond glacier, mountain high —
Oh, love is sweet at any price,
    As well know you and I!

51

So gayly the Northland took his heart
   And cast it in the wailing sea —
"Go, thou, with all thy cunning art,
   And woo my bride for me!"

For many a night and for many a day,
   And over the leagues that rolled between,
The true-heart messenger sped away
   To woo the Southland queen.

But the sea wailed loud, and the sea wailed
     long,
   While ever the Northland cried in glee:
"Oh, thou shalt sing us our bridal song,
   When comes my bride, O sea!"

At the foot of the Southland's golden throne
   The heart of the Northland ever throbs —
For that true-heart speaks in the waves that
     moan,
   The songs that it sings are sobs.

Ever the Southland spurns the cries
   Of the messenger pleading the Northland's
     part;
The summer shines in the Southland's eyes —
   The winter bides in her heart!

And ever unto that far-off place
   Which love doth render a hallowed spot,
The Northland turneth his honest face
   And wonders she cometh not.

The sea wails loud, and the sea wails long,
   As the ages of waiting drift slowly by,
But the sea shall sing no bridal song —
   As well know you and I!

HYMN

(FROM THE GERMAN OF MARTIN LUTHER)

O HEART of mine! lift up thine eyes
   And see who in yon manger lies!
Of perfect form, of face divine—
It is the Christ-child, heart of mine!

O dearest, holiest Christ-child, spread
Within this heart of mine thy bed;
Then shall my breast forever be
A chamber consecrate to thee!

Beat high to-day, O heart of mine,
And tell, O lips, what joys are thine;
For with your help shall I prolong
Old Bethlehem's sweetest cradle-song.

Glory to God, whom this dear Child
Hath by His coming reconciled,
And whose redeeming love again
Brings peace on earth, good will to men!

STAR OF THE EAST

STAR of the East, that long ago
　Brought wise men on their way
Where, angels singing to and fro,
　The Child of Bethlehem lay —
Above that Syrian hill afar
Thou shinest out to-night, O Star!

Star of the East, the night were drear
　But for the tender grace
That with thy glory comes to cheer
　Earth's loneliest, darkest place;
For by that charity we see
Where there is hope for all and me.

Star of the East! show us the way
　In wisdom undefiled
To seek that manger out and lay
　Our gifts before the child —
To bring our hearts and offer them
Unto our King in Bethlehem!

TWIN IDOLS

THERE are two phrases, you must know,
   So potent (yet so small)
That wheresoe'er a man may go
   He needs none else at all;
No servile guide to lead the way
   Nor lackey at his heel,
If he be learned enough to say
   " Comme bien " and " Wie viel."

The sleek, pomaded Parleyvoo
   Will air his sweetest airs
And quote the highest rates when you
   " Comme bien " for his wares;
And, though the German stolid be,
   His so-called heart of steel
Becomes as soft as wax when he
   Detects the words " Wie viel."

Go, search the boulevards and rues
    From Havre to Marseilles —
You 'll find all eloquence you use
    Except " Comme bien " fails;
Or in the country auf der Rhine
    Essay a business deal
And all your art is good fuhr nein
    Beyond the point — " Wie viel."

It matters not what game or prey
    Attracts your greedy eyes —
You must pursue the good old way
    If you would win the prize;
It is to get a titled mate
    All run down at the heel,
If you inquire of stock effete,
    " Comme bien " or " Wie viel."

So he is wise who envieth not
    A wealth of foreign speech,
Since with two phrases may be got
    Whatever 's in his reach;
For Europe is a soulless shrine
    In which all classes kneel
Before twin idols, deemed divine —
    " Comme bien " and " Wie viel."

TWO VALENTINES

I. — TO MISTRESS BARBARA

THERE were three cavaliers, all hand-
    some and true,
On Valentine's day came a maiden to woo,
And quoth to your mother: "Good-mor-
    row, my dear,
We came with some songs for your daugh-
    ter to hear!"

Your mother replied: "I 'll be pleased to
    convey
To my daughter what things you may sing
    or may say!"

Then the first cavalier sung: "My pretty red
    rose,
I 'll love you and court you some day, I sup-
    pose!"

And the next cavalier sung, with make-be-
    lieve tears:
"I 've loved you! I 've loved you these
    many long years!"

But the third cavalier (with the brown,
    bushy head
And the pretty blue jacket and necktie of
    red)
He drew himself up with a resolute air,
And he warbled: "O maiden, surpassingly
    fair!
I 've loved you long years, and I love you
    to-day,
And, if you will let me, I 'll love you for aye!"

I (the third cavalier) sang this ditty to you,
In my necktie of red and my jacket of blue;
I 'm sure you 'll prefer the song that was
    mine
And smile your approval on your valentine.

II.—TO A BABY BOY

Who I am I shall not say,
But I send you this bouquet

With this query, baby mine:
" Will you be my valentine ? "

See these roses blushing blue,
Very like your eyes of hue;
While these violets are the red
Of your cheeks.   It can be said
Ne'er before was babe like you.

And I think it is quite true
No one e'er before to-day
Sent so wondrous a bouquet
As these posies aforesaid —
Roses blue and violets red!

Sweet, repay me sweets for sweets —
'T is your lover who entreats!
Smile upon me, baby mine —
Be my little valentine!

MOTHER AND SPHINX

(EGYPTIAN FOLK-SONG)

GRIM is the face that looks into the night
　　Over the stretch of sands;
A sullen rock in a sea of white —
A ghostly shadow in ghostly light,
　　Peering and moaning it stands.
" Oh, is it the king that rides this way —
　　Oh, is it the king that rides so free?
I have looked for the king this many a day,
But the years that mock me will not say
　　Why tarrieth he! "

'T is not your king that shall ride to-night,
　　But a child that is fast asleep;
And the horse he shall ride is the Dream-
　　　horse white —
Aha, he shall speed through the ghostly
　　　light
　　Where the ghostly shadows creep!

" My eyes are dull and my face is sere,
  Yet unto the word he gave I cling,
For he was a Pharaoh that set me here —
And, lo! I have waited this many a year
  For him — my king!"

Oh, past thy face my darling shall ride
  Swift as the burning winds that bear
The sand clouds over the desert wide —
Swift to the verdure and palms beside
  The wells off there!
" And is it the mighty king I shall see
  Come riding into the night?
Oh, is it the king come back to me —
Proudly and fiercely rideth he,
  With centuries dight!"

I know no king but my dark-eyed dear
  That shall ride the Dream-Horse white;
But see! he wakes at my bosom here,
While the Dream-Horse frettingly lingers near
  To speed with my babe to-night!
And out of the desert darkness peers
  A ghostly, ghastly, shadowy thing
Like a spirit come out of the mouldering years,
And ever that waiting spectre hears
  The coming king!

62

A SPRING POEM FROM BION

ONE asketh:
    " Tell me, Myrson, tell me true:
What 's the season pleaseth you?
Is it summer suits you best,
When from harvest toil we rest?
  Is it autumn with its glory
    Of all surfeited desires?
  Is it winter, when with story
    And with song we hug our fires?
Or is spring most fair to you —
Come, good Myrson, tell me true!"

    Another answereth:
" What the gods in wisdom send
We should question not, my friend;
Yet, since you entreat of me,
I will answer reverently:

Me the summertime displeases,
    For its sun is scorching hot;
Autumn brings such dire diseases
    That perforce I like it not;
As for biting winter, oh!
How I hate its ice and snow!

" But, thrice welcome, kindly spring,
With the myriad gifts you bring!
Not too hot nor yet too cold,
Graciously your charms unfold —
    Oh, your days are like the dreaming
        Of those nights which love beseems,
    And your nights have all the seeming
        Of those days of golden dreams!
Heaven smiles down on earth, and then
Earth smiles up to heaven again!"

BÉRANGER'S "TO MY OLD COAT."

STILL serve me in my age, I pray,
 As in my youth, O faithful one;
For years I 've brushed thee every day —
 Could Socrates have better done?
What though the fates would wreak on thee
 The fulness of their evil art?
Use thou philosophy, like me —
 And we, old friend, shall never part!

I think — I *often* think of it —
 The day we twain first faced the crowd;
My roistering friends impeached your fit,
 But you and I were very proud!
Those jovial friends no more make free
 With us (no longer new and smart),
But rather welcome you and me
 As loving friends that should not part.

65

The patch? Oh, yes — one happy night —
    "Lisette," says I, "it 's time to go"—
She clutched this sleeve to stay my flight,
    Shrieking: "What! leave so early? No!"
To mend the ghastly rent she 'd made,
    Three days she toiled, dear patient heart!
And I — right willingly I staid —
    Lisette decreed we should not part!

No incense ever yet profaned
    This honest, shiny warp of thine,
Nor hath a courtier's eye disdained
    Thy faded hue and quaint design;
Let servile flattery be the price
    Of ribbons in the royal mart —
A roadside posie shall suffice
    For us two friends that must not part!

Fear not the recklessness of yore
    Shall re-occur to vex thee now;
Alas, I am a youth no more —
    I 'm old and sere, and so art thou!
So bide with me unto the last
    And with thy warmth caress this heart
That pleads, by memories of the Past,
    That two such friends should never part!

BEN APFELGARTEN

THERE was a certain gentleman, Ben
 Apfelgarten called,
 Who lived way off in Germany a many
 years ago,
And he was very fortunate in being very
 bald
 And so was very happy he was so.
        He warbled all the day
        Such songs as only they
Who are very, very circumspect and very
 happy may;
        The people wondered why,
        As the years went gliding by,
They never heard him once complain or even
 heave a sigh!

The women of the province fell in love with
 genial Ben,
 Till (may be you can fancy it) the dickens
 was to pay

Among the callow students and the sober-
    minded men —
  With the women-folk a-cuttin' up that
    way!
        Why, they gave him turbans red
        To adorn his hairless head,
And knitted jaunty nightcaps to protect him
    when abed!
        In vain the rest demurred —
        Not a single chiding word
Those ladies deigned to tolerate — remon-
    strance was absurd!

Things finally got into such a very dreadful
    way
  That the others (oh, how artful) formed
    the politic design
To send him to the reichstag; so, one dull
    November day,
  They elected him a member from the
    Rhine!
        Then the other members said:
        "Gott im Himmel! what a head!"
But they marvelled when his speeches they
    listened to or read;

And presently they cried:
  "There must be heaps inside
Of the smooth and shiny cranium his con-
  stituents deride!"

Well, when at last he up 'nd died — long
  past his ninetieth year —
  The strangest and the most lugubrious
    funeral he had,
For women came in multitudes to weep
  upon his bier —
  The men all wond'ring why on earth the
    women had gone mad!
      And this wonderment increased
      Till the sympathetic priest
Inquired of those same ladies: "Why this
  fuss about deceased?"
      Whereupon were they appalled,
      For, as one, those women squalled:
"We doted on deceased for being bald —
  bald — bald!"

He was bald because his genius burnt that
  shock of hair away
  Which, elsewise, clogs one's keenness and
    activity of mind;

And (barring present company, of course)
  I 'm free to say
  That, after all, it 's intellect that captures
    womankind.
      At any rate, since then
      (With a precedent in Ben),
The women-folk have been in love with us
  bald-headed men!

A HEINE LOVE SONG

THE image of the moon at night
All trembling in the ocean lies,
But she, with calm and steadfast light,
  Moves proudly through the radiant skies.

How like the tranquil moon thou art —
  Thou fairest flower of womankind!
And, look, within my fluttering heart
  Thy image trembling is enshrined!

UHLAND'S "CHAPEL"

YONDER stands the hillside chapel
   Mid the evergreens and rocks,
All day long it hears the song
   Of the shepherd to his flocks.

Then the chapel bell goes tolling —
   Knelling for a soul that 's sped;
Silent and sad the shepherd lad
   Hears the requiem for the dead.

Shepherd, singers of the valley,
   Voiceless now, speed on before;
Soon shall knell that chapel bell
   For the songs you 'll sing no more.

THE DREAMS

TWO dreams came down to earth one
night
  From the realm of mist and dew;
One was a dream of the old, old days,
  And one was a dream of the new.

One was a dream of a shady lane
  That led to the pickerel pond
Where the willows and rushes bowed them-
    selves
  To the brown old hills beyond.

And the people that peopled the old-time
    dream
  Were pleasant and fair to see,
And the dreamer he walked with them again
  As often of old walked he.

Oh, cool was the wind in the shady lane
    That tangled his curly hair!
Oh, sweet was the music the robins made
    To the springtime everywhere!

Was it the dew the dream had brought
    From yonder midnight skies,
Or was it tears from the dear, dead years
    That lay in the dreamer's eyes?

The *other* dream ran fast and free,
    As the moon benignly shed
Her golden grace on the smiling face
    In the little trundle-bed.

For 't was a dream of times to come —
    Of the glorious noon of day —
Of the summer that follows the careless
    spring
When the child is done with play.

And 't was a dream of the busy world
    Where valorous deeds are done;
Of battles fought in the cause of right,
    And of victories nobly won.

It breathed no breath of the dear old home
  And the quiet joys of youth;
It gave no glimpse of the good old friends
  Or the old-time faith and truth.

But 't was a dream of youthful hopes,
  And fast and free it ran,
And it told to a little sleeping child
  Of a boy become a man!

These were the dreams that came one night
  To earth from yonder sky;
These were the dreams two dreamers
    dreamed —
  My little boy and I.

And in our hearts my boy and I
  Were glad that it was so;
He loved to dream of days to come,
  And *I* of long ago.

So from our dreams my boy and I
  Unwillingly awoke,
But neither of his precious dream
  Unto the other spoke.

Yet of the love we bore those dreams
　Gave each his tender sign;
For there was triumph in *his* eyes —
　And there were tears in *mine !*

IN NEW ORLEANS

'T WAS in the Crescent City not long ago
    befell
The tear-compelling incident I now propose
    to tell;
So come, my sweet collector friends, and
    listen while I sing
Unto your delectation this brief, pathetic
    thing —
No lyric pitched in vaunting key, but just a
    requiem
Of blowing twenty dollars in by nine o'clock
    a. m.

Let critic folk the poet's use of vulgar slang
    upbraid,
But, when I 'm speaking by the card, I call
    a spade a spade;

And I, who have been touched of that same
    mania, myself,
Am well aware that, when it comes to part-
    ing with his pelf,
The curio collector is so blindly lost in sin
That he does n't spend his money — he sim-
    ply blows it in!

In Royal street (near Conti) there 's a lovely
    curio-shop,
And there, one balmy, fateful morn, it was
    my chance to stop;
To stop was hesitation — in a moment I was
    lost—
That kind of hesitation does not hesitate at
    cost!
I spied a pewter tankard there, and, my! it
    was a gem —
And the clock in old St. Louis told the hour
    of eight a. m.!

Three quaint Bohemian bottles, too, of yel-
    low and of green,
Cut in archaic fashion that I ne'er before had
    seen;

A lovely, hideous platter wreathed about
    with pink and rose,
With its curious depression into which the
    gravy flows;
Two dainty silver salts—oh, there was no
    resisting *them* —
And I 'd blown in twenty dollars by nine
    o'clock a. m.

With twenty dollars, one who is a prudent
    man, indeed,
Can buy the wealth of useful things his wife
    and children need;
Shoes, stockings, knickerbockers, gloves,
    bibs, nursing-bottles, caps,
A gown—*the* gown for which his spouse
    too long has pined, perhaps!
These and ten thousand other spectres har-
    row and condemn
The man who 's blown in twenty by nine
    o 'clock a. m.

Oh, mean advantage conscience takes (and
    one that I abhor!)
In asking one this question: "What *did* you
    buy it for?"

Why does n't conscience ply its blessed
  trade *before* the act,
Before one's cussedness becomes a bald, ac-
  complished fact —
Before one's fallen victim to the Tempter's
  stratagem
And blown in twenty dollars by nine o'clock
  a. m.?

Ah me! now that the deed is done, how
  penitent I am!
I *was* a roaring lion — behold a bleating
  lamb!
I 've packed and shipped those precious
  things to that more precious wife
Who shares with our sweet babes the
  strange vicissitudes of life,
While he who, in his folly, gave up his store
  of wealth
Is far away, and means to keep his distance
  — for his health!

MY PLAYMATES

THE wind comes whispering to me of
  the country green and cool—
Of redwing blackbirds chattering beside a
  reedy pool;
It brings me soothing fancies of the homestead on the hill,
And I hear the thrush's evening song and
  the robin's morning trill;
So I fall to thinking tenderly of those I used
  to know
Where the sassafras and snakeroot and
  checkerberries grow.

What has become of Ezra Marsh, who lived
  on Baker's hill?
And what 's become of Noble Pratt, whose
  father kept the mill?

And what 's become of Lizzie Crum and
    Anastasia Snell,
And of Roxie Root, who 'tended school in
    Boston for a spell ?
They were the boys and they the girls who
    shared my youthful play —
They do not answer to my call!   My play-
    mates — where are they ?

What has become of Levi and his little
    brother Joe,
Who lived next door to where we lived
    some forty years ago ?
I 'd like to see the Newton boys and Quincy
    Adams Brown,
And Hepsy Hall and Ella Cowles, who spelled
    the whole school down!
And Gracie Smith, the Cutler boys, Leander
    Snow, and all
Who I am sure would answer could they
    only hear my call!

I 'd like to see Bill Warner and the Conkey
    boys again
And talk about the times we used to wish
    that we were men!

And one — I shall not name her — could I
see her gentle face
And hear her girlish treble in this distant,
lonely place!
The flowers and hopes of springtime — they
perished long ago,
And the garden where they blossomed is
white with winter snow.

O cottage neath the maples, have you seen
those girls and boys
That but a little while ago made, oh! such
pleasant noise?
O trees, and hills, and brooks, and lanes, and
meadows, do you know
Where I shall find my little friends of forty
years ago?
You see I'm old and weary, and I've trav-
eled long and far;
I am looking for my playmates — I wonder
where they are!

STOVES AND SUNSHINE

PRATE, ye who will, of so-called charms
    you find across the sea —
The land of stoves and sunshine is good
    enough for me!
I 've done the grand for fourteen months in
    every foreign clime,
And I 've learned a heap of learning, but I 've
    shivered all the time;
And the biggest bit of wisdom I 've acquired
    — as I can see —
Is that which teaches that this land's the
    land of lands for me.

Now, I am of opinion that a person should
    get some
Warmth in this present life of ours, not all
    in that to come;

So when Boreas blows his blast, through
    country and through town,
Or when upon the muddy streets the stifling
    fog rolls down,
Go, guzzle in a pub, or plod some bleak
    malarious grove,
But let me toast my shrunken shanks beside
    some Yankee stove.

The British people say they "don't believe
    in stoves, y' know;"
Perchance because we warmed 'em so com-
    pletely years ago!
They talk of "drahfts" and "stuffiness" and
    "ill effects of heat,"
As they chatter in their barny rooms or
    shiver 'round the street;
With sunshine such a rarity, and stoves es-
    teemed a sin,
What wonder they are wedded to their fads
    — catarrh and gin ?

In Germany are stoves galore, and yet you
    seldom find
A fire within the stoves, for German stoves
    are not that kind;

The Germans say that fires make dirt, and
dirt 's an odious thing,
But the truth is that the pfennig is the aver-
age Teuton's king,
And since the fire costs pfennigs, why, the
thrifty soul denies
Himself all heat except what comes with
beer and exercise.

The Frenchman builds a fire of cones, the
Irishman of peat;
The frugal Dutchman buys a fire when he
has need of heat —
That is to say, he pays so much each day to
one who brings
The necessary living coals to warm his soup
and things;
In Italy and Spain they have no need to heat
the house —
'Neath balmy skies the native picks the
mandolin and louse.

Now, we 've no mouldy catacombs, no feu-
dal castles grim,
No ruined monasteries, no abbeys ghostly
dim;

86

Our ancient history is new, our future 's all
    ahead,
And we 've got a tariff bill that 's made all
    Europe sick abed —
But what is best, though short on tombs
    and academic groves,
We double discount Christendom on sun-
    shine and on stoves.

Dear land of mine! I come to you from
    months of chill and storm,
Blessing the honest people whose hearts and
    hearths are warm;
A fairer, sweeter song than this I mean to
    weave to you
When I 've reached my lakeside 'dobe and
    once get heated through;
But, even then, the burthen of that fairer
    song shall be
That the land of stoves and sunshine is good
    enough for me.

A DRINKING SONG

COME, brothers, share the fellowship
　　We celebrate to-night;
There 's grace of song on every lip
　　And every heart is light!
But first, before our mentor chimes
　　The hour of jubilee,
Let 's drink a health to good old times,
　　And good times yet to be!
　　　　　Clink, clink, clink!
　　　　　Merrily let us drink!
　　　　　　There 's store of wealth
　　　　　　And more of health
　　　　　In every glass, we think.
　　　　　Clink, clink, clink!
　　　　　To fellowship we drink!
　　　　　　And from the bowl
　　　　　　No genial soul
　　　　　In such an hour can shrink.

And you, oh, friends from west and east
   And other foreign parts,
Come share the rapture of our feast,
   The love of loyal hearts;
And in the wassail that suspends
   All matters burthensome,
We 'll drink a health to good old friends
.   And good friends yet to come.
       Clink, clink, clink!
       To fellowship we drink!
         And from the bowl
         No genial soul
       In such an hour will shrink.
       Clink, clink, clink!
       Merrily let us drink!
         There 's fellowship
         In every sip
       Of friendship's brew, we think.

THE LIMITATIONS OF YOUTH

I 'D like to be a cowboy an' ride a fiery
      hoss
   Way out into the big an' boundless west;
I 'd kill the bears an' catamounts an' wolves
      I come across,
   An' I 'd pluck the bal' head eagle from his
      nest!
            With my pistols at my side,
            I would roam the prarers wide,
An' to scalp the savage Injun in his wigwam
      would I ride —
            If I darst; but I darse n't!

I 'd like to go to Afriky an' hunt the lions
      there,
   An' the biggest ollyfunts you ever saw!

I would track the fierce gorilla to his equa-
　　torial lair,
　An' beard the cannybull that eats folks
　　raw!
　　　　I 'd chase the pizen snakes
　　　　An' the 'pottimus that makes
His nest down at the bottom of unfathom-
　　able lakes —
　　　　　If I darst; but I darse n't!

I would I were a pirut to sail the ocean blue,
　With a big black flag aflyin' overhead;
I would scour the billowy main with my gal-
　　lant pirut crew
　An' dye the sea a gouty, gory red!
　　　　With my cutlass in my hand
　　　　On the quarterdeck I 'd stand
And to deeds of heroism I 'd incite my pirut
　　band —
　　　　　If I darst; but I darse n't!

And, if I darst, I 'd lick my pa for the times
　　that he 's licked me!
　I 'd lick my brother an' my teacher, too!
I 'd lick the fellers that call round on sister
　　after tea,

An' I 'd keep on lickin' folks till I got
    through!
        You bet! I 'd run away
        From my lessons to my play,
An' I 'd shoo the hens, an' tease the cat, an'
    kiss the girls all day —
        If I darst; but I darse n't!

THE BOW-LEG BOY

WHO should come up the road one
day
But the doctor-man in his two-wheel shay!
And he whoaed his horse and he cried
"Ahoy!
I have brought you folks a bow-leg boy!
Such a cute little boy!
Such a funny little boy!
Such a dear little bow-leg boy!"

He took out his box and he opened it wide,
And there was the bow-leg boy inside!
And when they saw that cunning little mite,
They cried in a chorus expressive of delight:
"What a cute little boy!
What a funny little boy!
What a dear little bow-leg boy!"

93

Observing a strict geometrical law,
They cut out his panties with a circular saw;
Which gave such a stress to his oval stride
That the people he met invariably cried:
   "What a cute little boy!
      What a funny little boy!
         What a dear little bow-leg boy!"

They gave him a wheel and away he went
Speeding along to his heart's content;
And he sits so straight and he pedals so
    strong
That the folks all say as he bowls along:
   "What a cute little boy!
      What a funny little boy!
         What a dear little bow-leg boy!"

With his eyes aflame and his cheeks aglow,
He laughs "aha" and he laughs "oho";
And the world is filled and thrilled with the
    joy
Of that jolly little human, the bow-leg boy —
   The cute little boy!
      The funny little boy!
         The dear little bow-leg boy!

If ever the doctor-man comes *my* way
With his wonderful box in his two-wheel
    shay,
I 'll ask for the treasure I 'd fain possess —
Now, honest Injun! can't you guess?
    Why, a cute little boy —
        A funny little boy —
        A dear little bow-leg boy!

THE STRAW PARLOR

WAY up at the top of a big stack of
straw
Was the cunningest parlor that ever you
saw!
And there could you lie when aweary of play
And gossip or laze in the coziest way;
No matter how careworn or sorry one's
mood
No worldly distraction presumed to intrude.
As a refuge from onerous mundane ado
I think I approve of straw parlors, don't
you?

A swallow with jewels aflame on her breast
On that straw parlor's ceiling had builded
her nest;
And she flew in and out all the happy day
long,
And twittered the soothingest lullaby song.

Now some might suppose that that beautiful bird
Performed for her babies the music they
heard;
I reckon she twittered her répertoire through
For the folk in the little straw parlor, don't
you?

And down from a rafter a spider had hung
Some swings upon which he incessantly
swung.
He cut up such didoes — such antics he
played
Way up in the air, and was never afraid!
He never made use of his horrid old sting,
But was just upon earth for the fun of the
thing!
I deeply regret to observe that so few
Of these good-natured insects are met with,
don't you?

And, down in the strawstack, a wee little
mite
Of a cricket went chirping by day and by
night;

And further down, still, a cunning blue
    mouse
In a snug little nook of that strawstack kept
    house!
When the cricket went "chirp," Miss
    Mousie would squeak
"Come in," and a blush would enkindle
    her cheek!
She thought — silly girl! 't was a beau come
    to woo,
But I guess it was only the cricket, don't
    you?

So the cricket, the mouse, and the motherly
    bird
Made as soothingsome music as ever you
    heard;
And, meanwhile, that spider by means of
    his swings
Achieved most astounding gyrations and
    things!
No wonder the little folk liked what they
    saw
And loved what they heard in that parlor of
    straw!

With the mercury up to 102
In the shade, I opine they just sizzled, don't
    you?

But once there invaded that Eden of straw
The evilest Feline that ever you saw!
She pounced on that cricket with rare
    promptitude
And she tucked him away where he 'd do
    the most good;
And then, reaching down to the nethermost
    house,
She deftly expiscated little Miss Mouse!
And, as for the Swallow, she shrieked and
    withdrew —
I rather admire her discretion, don't you?

Now listen: That evening a cyclone ob-
    tained,
And the mortgage was all on that farm that
    remained!
Barn, strawstack and spider — they all blew
    away,
And nobody knows where they 're at to this
    day!

And, as for the little straw parlor, I fear
It was wafted clean off this sublunary
  sphere!
I really incline to a hearty "boo-hoo"
When I think of this tragical ending, don't
  you?

A PITEOUS PLAINT

I CANNOT eat my porridge,
   I weary of my play;
No longer can I sleep at night,
   No longer romp by day!
Though forty pounds was once my weight,
   I 'm shy of thirty now;
I pine, I wither and I fade
   Through love of Martha Clow.

As she rolled by this morning
   I heard the nurse girl say:
" She weighs just twenty-seven pounds
   And she 's one year old to-day."
I threw a kiss that nestled
   In the curls upon her brow,
But she never turned to thank me —
   That bouncing Martha Clow!

She ought to know I love her,
   For I 've told her that I do;
And I 've brought her nuts and apples,
   And sometimes candy, too!
I 'd drag her in my little cart
   If her mother would allow
That delicate attention
   To her daughter, Martha Clow.

O Martha! pretty Martha!
   Will you always be so cold?
Will you always be as cruel
   As you are at one-year-old?
Must your two-year-old admirer
   Pine as hopelessly as now
For a fond reciprocation
   Of his love for Martha Clow?

You smile on Bernard Rogers
   And on little Harry Knott;
You play with them at peek-a-boo
   All in the Waller Lot!
Wildly I gnash my new-cut teeth
   And beat my throbbing brow,
When I behold the coquetry
   Of heartless Martha Clow!

I cannot eat my porridge,
   Nor for my play care I;
Upon the floor and porch and lawn
   My toys neglected lie;
But on the air of Halsted street
   I breathe this solemn vow:
" Though *she* be *false, I* will be true
   To pretty Martha Clow!"

THE DISCREET COLLECTOR

DOWN south there is a curio-shop
  Unknown to many men;
Thereat do I intend to stop
  When I am south again;
The narrow street through which to go —
  Aha! I know it well!
And may be you would like to know —
  But no — I will not tell!

'T is there to find the loveliest plates
  (The bluest of the blue!)
At such surprisingly low rates
  You 'd not believe it true!
And there is one Napoleon vase
  Of dainty Sèvres to sell—
I 'm sure you 'd like to know that place —
  But no — I will not tell!

Then, too, I know another shop
   Has old, old beds for sale,
With lovely testers up on top
   Carved in ornate detail;
And there are sideboards rich and rare,
   With fronts that proudly swell —
Oh, there are bargains waiting there,
   But where I will not tell!

And hark ! I know a bottle-man
   Smiling and debonair,
And he has promised me I can
   Choose of his precious ware!
In age and shape and color, too,
   His dainty goods excel —
Aha, my friends, if you but knew —
   But no! I will not tell!

A thousand other shops I know
   Where bargains can be got —
Where other folk would like to go
   Who have what I have not.
I let them hunt; I hold my mouth —
   Yes, though I know full well
Where lie the treasures of the south,
   I 'm not a going to tell!

A VALENTINE

YOUR gran'ma, in her youth, was quite
    As blithe a little maid as you.
And, though her hair is snowy white,
    Her eyes still have their maiden blue,
And on her cheeks, as fair as thine,
    Methinks a girlish blush would glow
If she recalled the valentine
    She got, ah! many years ago.

A valorous youth loved gran'ma then,
    And wooed her in that auld lang syne;
And first he told his secret when
    He sent the maid that valentine.
No perfumed page nor sheet of gold
    Was that first hint of love he sent,
But with the secret gran'pa told —
    " I love you " — gran'ma was content.

Go, ask your gran'ma, if you will,
　If—though her head be bowed and gray—
If—though her feeble pulse be chill—
　True love abideth not for aye;
By that quaint portrait on the wall,
　That smiles upon her from above,
Methinks your gran'ma can recall
　The sweet divinity of love.

Dear Elsie, here's no page of gold—
　No sheet embossed with cunning art—
But here's a solemn pledge of old:
　"I love you, love, with all my heart."
And if in what I send you here
　You read not all of love expressed,
Go—go to gran'ma, Elsie dear,
　And she will tell you all the rest!

THE WIND

(THE TALE)

COMETH the Wind from the garden,
   fragrant and full of sweet singing —
Under my tree where I sit cometh the Wind
   to confession.

"Out in the garden abides the Queen of the
   beautiful Roses —
Her do I love and to-night wooed her with
   passionate singing;
Told I my love in those songs, and answer
   she gave in her blushes —
She shall be bride of the Wind, and she is
   the Queen of the Roses!"

"Wind, there is spice in thy breath; thy
   rapture hath fragrance Sabæan!"

"Straight from my wooing I come — my lips
  are bedewed with her kisses —
My lips and my song and my heart are
  drunk with the rapture of loving!"

(THE SONG)

The Wind he loveth the red, red Rose,
  And he wooeth his love to wed:
    Sweet is his song
    The Summer long
  As he kisseth her lips so red;
And he recketh naught of the ruin wrought
  When the Summer of love is sped!

(AGAIN THE TALE)

Cometh the Wind from the garden, bitter
  with sorrow of winter.

"Wind, is thy love-song forgot?   Where-
  fore thy dread lamentations?"

Sigheth and moaneth the Wind: "Out of
  the desolate garden
Come I from vigils with ghosts over the
  grave of the Summer!"

"Thy breath that was fragrant anon with
    rapture of music and loving,
It grieveth all things with its sting and the
    frost of its wailing displeasure."

The Wind maketh ever more moan and
    ever it giveth this answer:
"My heart it is numb with the cold of the
    love that was born of the Summer—
I come from the garden all white with the
    wrath and the sorrow of Winter;
I have kissed the low, desolate tomb where
    my bride in her loveliness lieth
And the voice of the ghost in my heart is the
    voice that forever outcrieth!"

(AGAIN THE SONG)

The Wind he waileth the red, red Rose
    When the Summer of love is sped—
        He waileth above
        His lifeless love
    With her shroud of snow o'erspread—
Crieth such things as a true heart brings
    To the grave of its precious dead.

A PARAPHRASE

OUR Father who art in heaven, hallowed
   be Thy name;
Thy Kingdom come, Thy will be done on
   earth, in Heaven the same;
Give us this day our daily bread, and may
   our debts to heaven —
As we our earthly debts forgive — by Thee
   be all forgiven;
When tempted or by evil vexed, restore
   Thou us again,
And Thine be the Kingdom, the Power, and
   the Glory, forever and ever; amen.

WITH BRUTUS IN ST. JO

OF all the opry-houses then obtaining in
the West
The one which Milton Tootle owned was,
by all odds, the best;
Milt, being rich, was much too proud to run
the thing alone,
So he hired an " acting manager," a gruff
old man named Krone —
A stern, commanding man with piercing
eyes and flowing beard,
And his voice assumed a thunderous tone
when Jack and I appeared;
He said that Julius Cæsar had been billed a
week or so,
And would have to have some armies by the
time he reached St. Jo!

O happy days, when Tragedy still winged
    an upward flight,
When actors wore tin helmets and cambric
    robes at night!
O happy days, when sounded in the public's
    rapturous ears
The creak of pasteboard armor and the clash
    of wooden spears!
O happy times for Jack and me and that one
    other supe
That then and there did constitute the no-
    blest Roman's troop!
With togas, battle axes, shields, we made a
    dazzling show,
When we were Roman soldiers with Brutus
    in St. Jo!

We wheeled and filed and double-quicked
    wherever Brutus led,
The folks applauding what we did as much
    as what he said;
'T was work, indeed; yet Jack and I were
    willing to allow
'T was easier following Brutus than follow-
    ing father's plough;

And at each burst of cheering, our valor
    would increase —
We tramped a thousand miles that night, at
    fifty cents apiece!
For love of Art — not lust for gold — con-
    sumed us years ago,
When we were Roman soldiers with Brutus
    in St. Jo!

To-day, while walking in the Square, Jack
    Langrish says to me:
" My friend, the drama nowadays ain't what
    it used to be!
These farces and these comedies — how
    feebly they compare
With that mantle of the tragic art which
    Forrest used to wear!
My soul is warped with bitterness to think
    that you and I —
Co-heirs to immortality in seasons long
    gone by —
Now draw a paltry stipend from a Boston
    comic show,
We, who were Roman soldiers with Brutus
    in St. Jo!"

And so we talked and so we mused upon
    the whims of Fate
That had degraded Tragedy from its old,
    supreme estate;
And duly, at the Morton bar, we stigmatized
    the age
As sinfully subversive of the interests of the
    Stage!
For Jack and I were actors in the halcyon,
    palmy days
Long, long before the Hoyt school of farce
    became the craze;
Yet, as I now recall it, it was twenty years
    ago
That we were Roman soldiers with Brutus
    in St. Jo!

We were by birth descended from a race of
    farmer kings
Who had done eternal battle with grasshop-
    pers and things;
But the Kansas farms grew tedious — we
    pined for that delight
We read of in the *Clipper* in the barber's
    shop by night!

We would be actors — Jack and I — and so
   we stole away
From our native spot, Wathena, one dull
   September day,
And started for Missouri — ah, little did we
   know
We were going to train as soldiers with
   Brutus in St. Jo!

Our army numbered three in all — Marc An-
   tony's was four;
Our army hankered after fame, but Marc's
   was after gore!
And when we reached Philippi, at the out-
   set we were met
With an inartistic gusto I can never quite
   forget.
For Antony's overwhelming force of thump-
   ers seemed to be
Resolved to do "them Kansas jays" — and
   that meant Jack and me!
My lips were sealed but that it seems quite
   proper you should know
That Rome was nowhere in it at Philippi in
   St. Jo!

I 've known the slow-consuming grief and
      ostentatious pain
Accruing from McKean Buchanan's melan-
      choly Dane;
Away out West I 've witnessed Bandmann's
      peerless hardihood,
With Arthur Cambridge have I wrought
      where walking was not good;
In every phase of horror have I bravely
      borne my part,
And even on my uppers have I proudly
      stood for Art!
And, after all my suffering, it were not hard
      to show
That I got my allopathic dose with Brutus
      at St. Jo!

That army fell upon me in a most bewilder-
      ing rage
And scattered me and mine upon that his-
      trionic stage;
My toga rent, my helmet gone and smashed
      to smithereens,
They picked me up and hove me through
      whole centuries of scenes!

I sailed through Christian eras and mediæval
  gloom
And fell from Arden forest into Juliet's
  painted tomb!
Oh, yes, I travelled far and fast that night,
  and I can show
The scars of honest wounds I got with
  Brutus in St. Jo!

Ah me, old Davenport is gone, of fickle fame
  forgot,
And Barrett sleeps forever in a much neg-
  lected spot;
Fred Warde, the papers tell me, in far woolly
  western lands
Still flaunts the banner of high Tragic Art
  at one-night stands;
And Jack and I, in Charley Hoyt's Bostonian
  dramas wreak
Our vengeance on creation at some eensty
  dolls. per week.
By which you see that public taste has fallen
  mighty low
Since we fought as Roman soldiers with
  Brutus in St. Jo!

THE TWO LITTLE SKEEZUCKS

THERE were two little skeezucks who
  lived in the isle
  Of Boo in a southern sea;
They clambered and rollicked in heathenish
  style
  In the boughs of their cocoanut tree.
They did n't fret much about clothing and
  such
  And they recked not a whit of the ills
      That sometimes accrue
      From having to do
With tailor and laundry bills.

The two little skeezucks once heard of a
  Fair
  Far off from their native isle,
And they asked of King Fan if they might n't
  go there
  To take in the sights for awhile.

Now old King Fan
Was a good-natured man
(As good-natured monarchs go),
And howbeit he swore that all Fairs were a
      bore,
He had n't the heart to say "No."

So the two little skeezucks sailed off to the
      Fair
  In a great big gum canoe,
And I fancy they had a good time there,
  For they tarried a year or two.
And old King Fan at last began
  To reckon they 'd come to grief,
      When glory! one day
      They sailed into the bay
To the tune of " Hail to the Chief!"

The two little skeezucks fell down on the
      sand,
  Embracing his majesty's toes,
Till his majesty graciously bade them stand
  And salute him nose to nose.
      And then quoth he:
      "Divulge unto me

What happenings have hapt to you;
And how did they dare to indulge in a Fair
So far from the island of Boo ?"

The two little skeezucks assured their king
  That what he surmised was true;
That the Fair would have been a different
    thing
  Had it only been held in Boo!
"The folk over there in no wise compare
With the folk of the southern seas;
      Why, they comb out their heads
      And they sleep in beds
Instead of in caverns and trees!"

The two little skeezucks went on to say
  That children (so far as they knew)
Had a much harder time in that land far away
  Than here in the island of Boo!
      They have to wear clo'es
      Which (as every one knows)
  Are irksome to primitive laddies,
While, with forks and with spoons, they're
  denied the sweet boons
  That accrue from free use of one's pad-
    dies!

"And now that you 're speaking of things
        to eat,"
    Interrupted the monarch of Boo,
"We beg to inquire if you happened to
        meet
    With a nice missionary or two?"
"No, that we did not; in that curious spot
    Where were gathered the fruits of the
        earth,
            Of that special kind
            Which Your Nibs has in mind
There appeared a deplorable dearth!"

Then loud laughed that monarch in heath-
        enish mirth
    And loud laughed his courtiers, too,
And they cried: "There is elsewhere no
        land upon earth
    So good as our island of Boo!"
            And the skeezucks, tho' glad
            Of the journey they 'd had,
    Climbed up in their cocoanut trees,
Where they still may be seen with no shirts
        to keep clean
Or trousers that bag at the knees.

PAN LIVETH

THEY told me once that Pan was dead,
  And so, in sooth, I thought him;
For vainly where the streamlets led
  Through flowery meads I sought him —
Nor in his dewy pasture bed
  Nor in the grove I caught him.
    " Tell me," 't was so my clamor ran —
    " Tell me, oh, where is Pan ?"

But, once, as on my pipe I played
  A requiem sad and tender,
Lo, thither came a shepherd-maid —
  Full comely she and slender !
I were indeed a churlish blade
  With wailings to offend 'er —
    For, surely, wooing's sweeter than
    A mourning over Pan!

123

So, presently, whiles I did scan
  That shepherd-maiden pretty,
And heard her accents, I began
  To pipe a cheerful ditty;
And so, betimes, forgot old Pan
  Whose death had waked my pity;
    So — so did Love undo the man
    Who sought and pined for Pan!

He was *not* dead! I found him there —
  The Pan that I was after!
Caught in that maiden's tangling hair,
  Drunk with her song and laughter!
I doubt if there be otherwhere
  A merrier god or dafter —
    Nay, nor a mortal kindlier than
    Is this same dear old Pan!

Beside me, as my pipe I play,
  My shepherdess is lying,
While here and there her lambkins stray
  As sunny hours go flying;
They look like me — those lambs — they say,
  And that I'm not denying!
    And for that sturdy, romping clan,
    All glory be to Pan!

124

Pan is not dead, O sweetheart mine!
  It is to hear his voices
In every note and every line
  Wherein the heart rejoices!
He liveth in that sacred shrine
  That Love's first, holiest choice is!
    So pipe, my pipe, while still you can,
    Sweet songs in praise of Pan!

DR. SAM

TO MISS GRACE KING

DOWN in the old French quarter,
　Just out of Rampart street,
　　I wend my way
　　At close of day
　　Unto the quaint retreat
Where lives the Voodoo Doctor
　By some esteemed a sham,
Yet I 'll declare there 's none elsewhere
　So skilled as Doctor Sam
　　　With the claws of a deviled crawfish,
　　　The juice of the prickly prune,
　　　And the quivering dew
　　　From a yarb that grew
　　　In the light of a midnight moon!

126

I never should have known him
  But for the colored folk
    That here obtain
    And ne'er in vain
  That wizard's art invoke;
For when the Eye that 's Evil
  Would him and his'n damn,
The negro's grief gets quick relief
  Of Hoodoo-Doctor Sam.
    With the caul of an alligator,
      The plume of an unborn loon,
        And the poison wrung
        From a serpent's tongue
      By the light of a midnight moon!

In all neurotic ailments
  I hear that he excels,
    And he insures
    Immediate cures
  Of weird, uncanny spells;
The most unruly patient
  Gets docile as a lamb
And is freed from ill by the potent skill
  Of Hoodoo-Doctor Sam;
    Feathers of strangled chickens,
      Moss from the dank lagoon,

127

And plasters wet
With spider sweat
In the light of a midnight moon!

They say when nights are grewsome
  And hours are, oh! so late,
    Old Sam steals out
    And hunts about
  For charms that hoodoos hate!
That from the moaning river
  And from the haunted glen
He silently brings what eerie things
  Give peace to hoodooed men: —
  The tongue of a piebald 'possum,
    The tooth of a senile 'coon,
  The buzzard's breath that smells of
      death,
    And the film that lies
    On a lizard's eyes
  In the light of a midnight moon!

WINFREDA

(A BALLAD IN THE ANGLO-SAXON TONGUE)

WHEN to the dreary greenwood gloam
  Winfreda's husband strode that day,
The fair Winfreda bode at home
  To toil the weary time away;
"While thou art gone to hunt," said she,
"I'll brew a goodly sop for thee."

Lo, from a further, gloomy wood,
  A hungry wolf all bristling hied
And on the cottage threshold stood
  And saw the dame at work inside;
And, as he saw the pleasing sight,
He licked his fangs so sharp and white.

Now when Winfreda saw the beast,
  Straight at the grinning wolf she ran,
And, not affrighted in the least,
  She hit him with her cooking pan,

And as she thwacked him on the head —
"Scat! scat!" the fair Winfreda said.

The hills gave answer to their din —
  The brook in fear beheld the sight.
And all that bloody field within
  Wore token of Winfreda's might.
The wolf was very loath to stay —
But, oh! he could not get away.

Winfreda swept him o'er the wold
  And choked him till his gums were blue,
And till, beneath her iron hold,
  His tongue hung out a yard or two,
And with his hair the riven ground
Was strewn for many leagues around.

They fought a weary time that day,
  And seas of purple blood were shed,
Till by Winfreda's cunning lay
  That awful wolf all limp and dead;
Winfreda saw him reel and drop —
Then back she went to brewing sop.

So when the husband came at night
  From bootless chase, cold, gaunt, and
    grim,
Great was that Saxon lord's delight
  To find the sop dished up for him;
And as he ate, Winfreda told
How she had laid the wolf out cold.

The good Winfreda of those days
  Is only "pretty Birdie" now —
Sickly her soul and weak her ways —
  And she, to whom we Saxons bow,
Leaps on a bench and screams with fright
If but a mouse creeps into sight.

LYMAN, FREDERICK, AND JIM

(FOR THE FELLOWSHIP CLUB)

LYMAN and Frederick and Jim, one day,
  Set out in a great big ship —
Steamed to the ocean adown the bay
  Out of a New York slip.
" Where are you going and what is your
    game ? "
  The people asked those three.
" Darned if we know; but all the same
  Happy as larks are we;
  And happier still we 're going to be ! "
        Said Lyman
        And Frederick
        And Jim.

The people laughed " Aha, oho!
  Oho, aha ! " laughed they;
And while those three went sailing so
  Some pirates steered that way.

The pirates they were laughing, too —
  The prospect made them glad;
But by the time the job was through
  Each of them pirates, bold and bad,
  Had been done out of all he had
          By Lyman
          And Frederick
          And Jim.

Days and weeks and months they sped,
  Painting that foreign clime
A beautiful, bright vermilion red —
  And having a —— of a time!
'T was all so gaudy a lark, it seemed
  As if it could not be,
And some folks thought it a dream they
    dreamed
  Of sailing that foreign sea,
  But I 'll identify you these three —
          Lyman
          And Frederick
          And Jim.

Lyman and Frederick are bankers and sich
  And Jim is an editor kind;

The first two named are awfully rich
   And Jim ain't far behind!
So keep your eyes open and mind your
     tricks,
   Or you are like to be
In quite as much of a Tartar fix
   As the pirates that sailed the sea
   And monkeyed with the pardners three,
         Lyman
         And Frederick
         And Jim!

BE MY SWEETHEART

SWEETHEART, be my sweetheart
  When birds are on the wing,
When bee and bud and babbling flood
  Bespeak the birth of spring,
Come, sweetheart, be my sweetheart
  And wear this posy-ring!

Sweetheart, be my sweetheart
  In the mellow golden glow
Of earth aflush with the gracious blush
  Which the ripening fields foreshow;
Dear sweetheart, be my sweetheart,
  As into the noon we go!

Sweetheart, be my sweetheart
  When falls the bounteous year,
When fruit and wine of tree and vine
  Give us their harvest cheer;
Oh, sweetheart, be my sweetheart,
  For winter it draweth near.

Sweetheart, be my sweetheart
  When the year is white and old,
When the fire of youth is spent, forsooth,
  And the hand of age is cold;
Yet, sweetheart, be my sweetheart
  Till the year of our love be told!

THE PETER-BIRD

OUT of the woods by the creek cometh
   a calling for Peter,
And from the orchard a voice echoes and
   echoes it over;
Down in the pasture the sheep hear that
   strange crying for Peter,
Over the meadows that call is aye and forever repeated.
So let me tell you the tale, when, where, and
   how it all happened,
And, when the story is told, let us pay heed
   to the lesson.

Once on a time, long ago, lived in the State
   of Kentucky
One that was reckoned a witch — full of
   strange spells and devices;
Nightly she wandered the woods, searching
   for charms voodooistic —

Scorpions, lizards, and herbs, dormice,
  chameleons, and plantains!
Serpents and caw-caws and bats, screech-
  owls and crickets and adders —
These were the guides of that witch through
  the dank deeps of the forest.
Then, with her roots and her herbs, back to
  her cave in the morning
Ambled that hussy to brew spells of unspeakable evil;
And, when the people awoke, seeing that
  hillside and valley
Sweltered in swathes as of mist — "Look!"
  they would whisper in terror —
"Look! the old witch is at work brewing
  her spells of great evil!"
Then would they pray till the sun, darting
  his rays through the vapor,
Lifted the smoke from the earth and baffled
  the witch's intentions.

One of the boys at that time was a certain
  young person named Peter,
Given too little to work, given too largely
  to dreaming;

Fonder of books than of chores, you can
imagine that Peter
Led a sad life on the farm, causing his par-
ents much trouble.
"Peter!" his mother would call, "the cream
is a'ready for churning!"
"Peter!" his father would cry, "go grub at
the weeds in the garden!"
So it was "Peter!" all day — calling, re-
minding, and chiding —
Peter neglected his work; therefore that nag-
ging at Peter!

Peter got hold of some books — how, I 'm
unable to tell you;
Some have suspected the witch — this is no
place for suspicions!
It is sufficient to stick close to the thread of
the legend.
Nor is it stated or guessed what was the
trend of those volumes;
What thing soever it was — done with a pen
and a pencil,
Wrought with a brain, not a hoe — surely
't was hostile to farming!

"Fudge on all readin'!" they quoth; or
    "*that's* what 's the ruin of Peter!"

So, when the mornings were hot, under the
    beech or the maple,
Cushioned in grass that was blue, breathing
    the breath of the blossoms,
Lulled by the hum of the bees, the coo of
    the ring-doves a-mating,
Peter would frivol his time at reading, or
    lazing, or dreaming.
"Peter!" his mother would call, "the
    cream is a'ready for churning!"
"Peter!" his father would cry, "go grub at
    the weeds in the garden!"
"Peter!" and "Peter!" all day — calling,
    reminding, and chiding —
Peter neglected his chores; therefore that
    outcry for Peter;
Therefore the neighbors allowed evil would
    surely befall him —
Yes, on account of these things, ruin would
    come upon Peter!

Surely enough, on a time, reading and laz-
    ing and dreaming

Wrought the calamitous ill all had predicted
    for Peter;
For, of a morning in spring when lay the
    mist in the valleys —
"See," quoth the folk, "how the witch
    breweth her evil decoctions!
See how the smoke from her fire broodeth
    on woodland and meadow!
Grant that the sun cometh out to smother
    the smudge of her caldron!
She hath been forth in the night, full of her
    spells and devices,
Roaming the marshes and dells for heathen-
    ish magical nostrums;
Digging in leaves and at stumps for centi-
    pedes, pismires, and spiders,
Grubbing in poisonous pools for hot sala-
    manders and toadstools;
Charming the bats from the flues, snaring
    the lizards by twilight,
Sucking the scorpion's egg and milking the
    breast of the adder!"

Peter derided these things held in such faith
    by the farmer,

Scouted at magic and charms, hooted at
    Jonahs and hoodoos —
Thinking and reading of books must have
    unsettled his reason!
"There ain't no witches," he cried; "it
    is n't smoky, but foggy!
I will go out in the wet — you all can't hen-
    der me, nuther!"

Surely enough he went out into the damp
    of the morning,
Into the smudge that the witch spread over
    woodland and meadow,
Into the fleecy gray pall brooding on hillside
    and valley.
Laughing and scoffing, he strode into that
    hideous vapor;
Just as he said he would do, just as he
    bantered and threatened,
Ere they could fasten the door, Peter had
    done gone and done it!
Wasting his time over books, you see, had
    unsettled his reason —
Soddened his callow young brain with semi-
    pubescent paresis,

And his neglect of his chores hastened this
    evil condition.

Out of the woods by the creek cometh a
    calling for Peter
And from the orchard a voice echoes and
    echoes it over;
Down in the pasture the sheep hear that
    shrill crying for Peter,
Up from the spring house the wail stealeth
    anon like a whisper,
Over the meadows that call is aye and for-
    ever repeated.
Such *were* the voices that whooped wildly
    and vainly for Peter
Decades and decades ago down in the State
    of Kentucky —
Such *are* the voices that cry now from the
    woodland and meadow,
" Peter—O Peter!" all day, calling, remind-
    ing, and chiding —
Taking us back to the time when Peter he
    done gone and done it!
These are the voices of those left by the boy
    in the farmhouse

143

When, with his laughter and scorn, hatless
and bootless and sockless,
Clothed in his jeans and his pride, Peter
sailed out in the weather,
Broke from the warmth of his home into
that fog of the devil,
Into the smoke of that witch brewing her
damnable porridge!

Lo, when he vanished from sight, knowing
the evil that threatened,
Forth with importunate cries hastened his
father and mother.
" Peter!" they shrieked in alarm, " Peter!"
and evermore " Peter!" —
Ran from the house to the barn, ran from the
barn to the garden,
Ran to the corn-crib anon, then to the
smoke-house proceeded;
Henhouse and woodpile they passed, calling
and wailing and weeping,
Through the front gate to the road, braving
the hideous vapor —
Sought him in lane and on pike, called him
in orchard and meadow,

Clamoring ''Peter!'' in vain, vainly outcry-
ing for Peter.
Joining the search came the rest, brothers
and sisters and cousins,
Venting unspeakable fears in pitiful wailing
for Peter!
And from the neighboring farms gathered
the men and the women,
Who, upon hearing the news, swelled the
loud chorus for Peter.

Farmers and hussifs and maids, bosses and
field-hands and niggers,
Colonels and jedges galore from cornfields
and mint-beds and thickets,
All that had voices to voice, all to those
parts appertaining,
Came to engage in the search, gathered and
bellowed for Peter.
The Taylors, the Dorseys, the Browns, the
Wallers, the Mitchells, the Logans,
The Yenowines, Crittendens, Dukes, the
Hickmans, the Hobbses, the Morgans;
The Ormsbys, the Thompsons, the Hikes,
the Williamsons, Murrays, and Hardins,

The Beynroths, the Sherleys, the Hokes, the
    Haldermans, Harneys, and Slaughters—
All, famed in Kentucky of old for prowess
    prodigious at farming,
Now surged from their prosperous homes
    to join in that hunt for the truant,
To ascertain where he was at, to help out
    the chorus for Peter.

Still on those prosperous farms where heirs
    and assigns of the people
Specified hereinabove and proved by the
    records of probate —
Still on those farms shall you hear (and still
    on the turnpikes adjacent)
That pitiful, petulant call, that pleading, ex-
    postulant wailing,
That hopeless, monotonous moan, that
    crooning and droning for Peter.
Some say the witch in her wrath trans-
    mogrified all those good people;
That, wakened from slumber that day by
    the calling and bawling for Peter,
She out of her cave in a thrice, and, waving
    the foot of a rabbit

146

(Crossed with the caul of a coon and
    smeared with the blood of a chicken),
She changed all those folk into birds and
    shrieked with demoniac venom:
"Fly away over the land, moaning your
    Peter forever,
Croaking of Peter, the boy who did n't be-
    lieve there were hoodoos,
Crooning of Peter, the fool who scouted at
    stories of witches,
Crying of Peter for aye, forever outcalling
    for Peter!"

This is the story they tell; so in good sooth
    saith the legend;
As I have told it to you, so tell the folk and
    the legend.
That it is true I believe, for on the breezes
    this morning
Come the shrill voices of birds calling and
    calling for Peter;
Out of the maple and beech glitter the eyes
    of the wailers,
Peeping and peering for him who formerly
    lived in these places —

Peter, the heretic lad, lazy and careless and
    dreaming,
Sorely afflicted with books and with pubes-
    cent paresis,
Hating the things of the farm, care of the
    barn and the garden,
Always neglecting his chores — given to
    books and to reading,
Which, as all people allow, turn the young
    person to mischief,
Harden his heart against toil, wean his affec-
    tions from tillage.

This is the legend of yore told in the state of
    Kentucky
When in the springtime the birds call from
    the beeches and maples,
Call from the petulant thorn, call from the
    acrid persimmon;
When from the woods by the creek and
    from the pastures and meadows,
When from the spring house and lane and
    from the mint-bed and orchard,
When from the redbud and gum and from
    the redolent lilac,

When from the dirt roads and pikes cometh
that calling for Peter;
Cometh the dolorous cry, cometh that weird
iteration
Of " Peter " and " Peter " for aye, of " Peter "
and " Peter " forever!
This is the legend of old, told in the tum-
titty meter
Which the great poets prefer, being less la-
bor than rhyming
(My first attempt at the same, my *last* attempt, too, I reckon!);
Nor have I further to say, for the sad story
is ended.

SISTER'S CAKE

I 'D not complain of Sister Jane, for she
was good and kind,
Combining with rare comeliness distinctive
gifts of mind;
Nay, I 'll admit it were most fit that, worn
by social cares,
She 'd crave a change from parlor life to that
below the stairs,
And that, eschewing needlework and music,
she should take
Herself to the substantial art of manufact-
uring cake.

At breakfast, then, it would befall that Sister
Jane would say:
"Mother, if you have got the things, I 'll
make some cake to-day!"

150

Poor mother 'd cast a timid glance at father,
    like as not —
For father hinted sister's cooking cost a
    frightful lot —
But neither *she* nor *he* presumed to signify
    dissent,
Accepting it for gospel truth that what she
    wanted went!

No matter what the rest of 'em might chance
    to have in hand,
The whole machinery of the house came to
    a sudden stand;
The pots were hustled off the stove, the fire
    built up anew,
With every damper set just so to heat the
    oven through;
The kitchen-table was relieved of everything,
    to make
That ample space which Jane required when
    she compounded cake.

And, oh! the bustling here and there, the
    flying to and fro;
The click of forks that whipped the eggs to
    lather white as snow —

And what a wealth of sugar melted swiftly
    out of sight —
And butter? Mother said such waste would
    ruin father, quite!
But Sister Jane preserved a mien no plead-
    ing could confound
As she utilized the raisins and the citron by
    the pound.

Oh, hours of chaos, tumult, heat, vexatious
    din, and whirl!
Of deep humiliation for the sullen hired-girl;
Of grief for mother, hating to see things
    wasted so,
And of fortune for that little boy who pined
    to taste that dough!
It looked so sweet and yellow — sure, to
    taste it were no sin —
But, oh! how sister scolded if he stuck his
    finger in!

The chances were as ten to one, before the
    job was through,
That sister'd think of something else she'd
    great deal rather do!

So, then, she 'd softly steal away, as Arabs
    in the night,
Leaving the girl and ma to finish up as best
    they might;
These tactics (artful Sister Jane) enabled her
    to take
Or shift the credit or the blame of that too-
    treacherous cake!

And yet, unhappy is the man who has no
    Sister Jane —
For he who has no sister seems to me to
    live in vain.
I never had a sister — may be that is why to-
    day
I 'm wizened and dyspeptic, instead of blithe
    and gay;
A boy who 's only forty should be full of
    romp and mirth,
But *I* (because I 'm sisterless) am the oldest
    man on earth!

Had I a little sister — oh, how happy I should
    be!
I 'd never let her cast her eyes on any chap
    but me;

I 'd love her and I 'd cherish her for better
and for worse —
I 'd buy her gowns and bonnets, and sing
her praise in verse;
And — yes, what 's more and vastly more —
I tell you what I 'd do:
I 'd let her make her wondrous cake, and I
would eat it, too!

I have a high opinion of the sisters, as you
see —
Another fellow's sister is so very dear to me!
I love to work anear her when she 's mak-
ing over frocks,
When she patches little trousers or darns
prosaic socks;
But I draw the line at one thing — yes, I don
my hat and take
A three hours' walk when she is moved to
try her hand at cake!

ABU MIDJAN

" *W*HEN Father Time swings round
        his scythe,
    Intomb me 'neath the bounteous vine,
So that its juices, red and blithe,
    May cheer these thirsty bones of mine.

" *Elsewise with tears and bated breath*
    Should I survey the life to be.
But oh!   How should I hail the death
    That brings that vinous grace to me!"

So sung the dauntless Saracen,
    Whereat the Prophet-Chief ordains
That, curst of Allah, loathed of men,
    The faithless one shall die in chains.

But one vile Christian slave that lay
    A prisoner near that prisoner saith :
"God willing, I will plant some day
    A vine where liest thou in death."

Lo, over Abu Midjan's grave
　With purpling fruit a vine-tree grows;
Where rots the martyred Christian slave
　Allah, and only Allah, knows!

ED

E^D was a man that played for keeps, 'nd
when he tuk the notion,
You cud n't stop him any more 'n a dam 'ud
stop the ocean;
For when he tackled to a thing 'nd sot his
mind plum to it,
You bet yer boots he done that thing though
it broke the bank to do it!
So all us boys uz knowed him best allowed
he wuz n't jokin'
When on a Sunday he remarked uz how
he 'd gin up smokin'.

Now this remark, that Ed let fall, fell, ez I
say, on Sunday —
Which is the reason we wuz shocked to see
him sail in Monday

A-puffin' at a snipe that sizzled like a Chi-
nese cracker
An' smelt fur all the world like rags instead
uv like terbacker;
Recoverin' from our first surprise, us fellows
fell to pokin'
A heap uv fun at "folks uz said how they
had gin up smokin'."

But Ed — sez he: "I found my work cud
not be done without it —
Jes' try the scheme yourselves, my friends,
ef any uv you doubt it!
It's hard, I know, upon one's health, but
there's a certain beauty
In makin' sackerfices to the stern demands
uv duty!
So, wholly in a sperrit uv denial 'nd conces-
sion,
I mortify the flesh 'nd smoke for the sake uv
my perfession!"

JENNIE

SOME men affect a liking
   For the prim in face and mind,
And some prefer the striking
   And the loud in womankind;
Wee Madge is wooed of many,
   And buxom Kate, as well,
And Jennie — charming Jennie —
   Ah, Jennie does n't tell!

What eyes so bright as Daisy's,
   And who as Maud so fair?
Who does not sing the praises
   Of Lucy's golden hair?
There 's Sophie — she is witty,
   A very sprite is Nell,
And Susie's, oh, so pretty —
   But Jennie does n't tell!

And now for my confession:
  Of all the virtues rare,
I argue that discretion
  Doth most beseem the fair.
And though I hear the many
  Extol each other belle,
I — I pronounce for Jennie,
  For Jennie does n't tell!

CONTENTMENT

HAPPY the man that, when his day is
    done,
   Lies down to sleep with nothing of re-
    gret —
The battle he has fought may not be won —
   The fame he sought be just as fleeting yet;
Folding at last his hands upon his breast,
   Happy is he, if hoary and forespent,
He sinks into the last, eternal rest,
   Breathing these only words: "I am con-
    tent."

But happier he, that, while his blood is warm,
   Sees hopes and friendships dead about him
    lie —
Bares his brave breast to envy's bitter storm,
   Nor shuns the poison barbs of calumny;
And 'mid it all, stands sturdy and elate,
   Girt only in the armor God hath meant
For him who 'neath the buffetings of fate
   Can say to God and man: "I am content."

"GUESS"

THERE is a certain Yankee phrase
    I always have revered,
Yet, somehow, in these modern days,
    It 's almost disappeared;
It was the usage years ago,
    But nowadays it 's got
To be regarded coarse and low
      To answer: "I guess not!"

The height of fashion called the pink
    Affects a British craze —
Prefers "I fancy" or "I think"
    To that time-honored phrase;
But here 's a Yankee, if you please,
    That brands the fashion rot,
And to all heresies like these
      He answers, "I — guess not!" —

When Chaucer, Wycliff, and the rest
    Express their meaning thus,
I guess, if not the very best,
    It 's good enough for us!
Why! shall the idioms of our speech
    Be banished and forgot
For this vain trash which moderns teach?
    Well, no, sir; I guess not!

There 's meaning in that homely phrase
    No other words express —
No substitute therefor conveys
    Such unobtrusive stress.
True Anglo-Saxon speech, it goes
    Directly to the spot,
And he who hears it always knows
    The worth of " I — guess — not!"

NEW-YEAR'S EVE

GOOD old days — dear old days
　　When my heart beat high and bold —
When the things of earth seemed full of
　　　life,
　　And the future a haze of gold!
Oh, merry was I that winter night,
　　And gleeful our little one's din,
And tender the grace of my darling's face
　　As we watched the new year in.
But a voice — a spectre's, that mocked at
　　　love —
　　Came out of the yonder hall;
"Tick-tock, tick-tock!" 't was the solemn
　　　clock
　　That ruefully croaked to all.
Yet what knew we of the griefs to be
　　In the year we longed to greet?
Love — love was the theme of the sweet,
　　　sweet dream
　　I fancied might never fleet!

But the spectre stood in that yonder gloom,
   And these were the words it spake,
" Tick-tock, tick-tock " — and they seemed
     to mock
   A heart about to break.

'T is new-year's eve, and again I watch
   In the old familiar place,
And I 'm thinking again of that old time
     when
   I looked on a dear one's face.
Never a little one hugs my knee
   And I hear no gleeful shout —
I am sitting alone by the old hearthstone,
   Watching the old year out.
But I welcome the voice in yonder gloom
   That solemnly calls to me:
" Tick-tock, tick-tock! " — for so the clock
   Tells of a life to be;
" Tick-tock, tick-tock! "—'t is so the clock
   Tells of eternity.

OLD SPANISH SONG

I 'M thinking of the wooing
   That won my maiden heart
When he — he came pursuing
   A love unused to art.
Into the drowsy river
   The moon transported flung
Her soul that seemed to quiver
   With the songs my lover sung.
And the stars in rapture twinkled
   On the slumbrous world below —
You see that, old and wrinkled,
   I 'm not forgetful — no!

He still should be repeating
   The vows he uttered then —
Alas! the years, though fleeting,
   Are truer yet than men!

The summer moonlight glistens
  In the favorite trysting spot
Where the river ever listens
  For a song it heareth not.
And I, whose head is sprinkled
  With time's benumbing snow,
I languish, old and wrinkled,
  But not forgetful — no!

What though he elsewhere turneth
  To beauty strangely bold?
Still in my bosom burneth
  The tender fire of old;
And the words of love he told me
  And the songs he sung me then
Come crowding to uphold me,
  And I live my youth again!
For when love's feet have tinkled
  On the pathway women go,
Though one be old and wrinkled,
  She 's not forgetful — no!

THE BROKEN RING

TO the willows of the brookside
   The mill wheel sings to-day —
     Sings and weeps,
     As the brooklet creeps
   Wondering on its way;
And here is the ring *she* gave me
   With love's sweet promise then —
     It hath burst apart
     Like the trusting heart
   That may never be soothed again!

Oh, I would be a minstrel
   To wander far and wide,
Weaving in song the merciless wrong
   Done by a perjured bride!
Or I would be a soldier,
   To seek in the bloody fray
What gifts of fate can compensate
   For the pangs I suffer to-day!

Yet may this aching bosom,
  By bitter sorrow crushed,
    Be still and cold
    In the churchyard mould
  Ere *thy* sweet voice be hushed;
So sing, sing on forever,
  O wheel of the brookside mill,
    For you mind me again
    Of the old time when
  I felt love's gracious thrill.

IN PRAISE OF CONTENTMENT

(HORACE'S ODES, III, I)

I HATE the common, vulgar herd!
  Away they scamper when I " booh " 'em!
But pretty girls and nice young men
Observe a proper silence when
  I chose to sing my lyrics to 'em.

The kings of earth, whose fleeting pow'r
  Excites our homage and our wonder,
Are precious small beside old Jove,
The father of us all, who drove
  The giants out of sight, by thunder!

This man loves farming, that man law,
  While this one follows pathways martial—
What moots it whither mortals turn?
Grim fate from her mysterious urn
  Doles out the lots with hand impartial.

Nor sumptuous feasts nor studied sports
   Delight the heart by care tormented;
The mightiest monarch knoweth not
The peace that to the lowly cot
   Sleep bringeth to the swain contented.

On him untouched of discontent
   Care sits as lightly as a feather;
He does n't growl about the crops,
Or worry when the market drops,
   Or fret about the changeful weather.

Not so with him who, rich in fact,
   Still seeks his fortune to redouble;
Though dig he deep or build he high,
Those scourges twain shall lurk anigh —
   Relentless Care, relentless Trouble!

If neither palaces nor robes
   Nor unguents nor expensive toddy
Insure Contentment's soothing bliss,
Why should I build an edifice
   Where Envy comes to fret a body?

Nay, I 'd not share your sumptuous cheer,
  But rather sup my rustic pottage,
While that sweet boon the gods bestow —
The peace your mansions cannot know —
  Blesseth my lowly Sabine cottage.

THE BALLAD OF THE TAYLOR PUP

N OW lithe and listen, gentles all,
  Now lithe ye all and hark
Unto a ballad I shall sing
  About Buena Park.

Of all the wonders happening there
  The strangest hap befell
Upon a famous Aprile morn,
  As I you now shall tell.

It is about the Taylor pup
  And of his mistress eke
And of the prankish time they had
  That I am fain to speak.

FITTE THE FIRST

The pup was of as noble mien
  As e'er you gazed upon;

They called his mother Lady
  And his father was a Don.

And both his mother and his sire
  Were of the race Bernard —
The family famed in histories
  And hymned of every bard.

His form was of exuberant mold,
  Long, slim, and loose of joints;
There never yet was pointer-dog
  So full as he of points.

His hair was like to yellow fleece,
  His eyes were black and kind,
And like a nodding, gilded plume
  His tail stuck up behind.

His bark was very, very fierce,
  And fierce his appetite,
Yet was it only things to eat
  That he was prone to bite.

But in that one particular
  He was so passing true
That never did he quit a meal
  Until he had got through.

Potatoes, biscuits, mush or hash,
  Joint, chop, or chicken limb —
So long as it was edible,
  'T was all the same to him!

And frequently when Hunger's pangs
  Assailed that callow pup,
He masticated boots and gloves
  Or chewed a door-mat up.

So was he much beholden of
  The folk that him did keep;
They loved him when he was awake
  And better still asleep.

FITTE THE SECOND

Now once his master, lingering o'er
  His breakfast coffee-cup,
Observed unto his doting spouse:
  "You ought to wash the pup!"

"That shall I do this very day,
  His doting spouse replied;
"You will not know the pretty thing
  When he is washed and dried.

" But tell me, dear, before you go
    Unto your daily work,
Shall I use Ivory soap on him,
    Or Colgate, Pears' or Kirk ? "

"Odzooks, it matters not a whit —
    They all are good to use!
Take Pearline, if it pleases you —
    Sapolio, if you choose!

"Take any soap, but take the pup
    And also water take,
And mix the three discreetly up
    Till they a lather make.

"Then mixing these constituent parts,
    Let Nature take her way,"
With which advice that sapient sir
    Had nothing more to say.

Then fared he to his daily toil
    All in the Board of Trade,
While Mistress Taylor for that bath
    Due preparation made.

FITTE THE THIRD

She whistled gayly to the pup
   And called him by his name,
And presently the guileless thing
   All unsuspecting came.

But when she shut the bath-room door,
   And caught him as catch-can,
And hove him in that odious tub,
   His sorrows then began.

How did that callow, yallow thing
   Regret that Aprile morn —
Alas! how bitterly he rued
   The day that he was born!

Twice and again, but all in vain
   He lifted up his wail;
His voice was all the pup could lift,
   For thereby hangs this tale.

'T was by that tail she held him down,
   And presently she spread
The creamy lather on his back,
   His stomach, and his head.

His ears hung down in sorry wise,
　　His eyes were, oh! so sad —
He looked as though he just had lost
　　The only friend he had.

And higher yet the water rose,
　　The lather still increased,
And sadder still the countenance
　　Of that poor martyred beast!

Yet all the time his mistress spoke
　　Such artful words of cheer
As "Oh, how nice!" and "Oh, how
　　clean!"
And "There's a patient dear!"

At last the trial had an end,
　　At last the pup was free;
She threw aside the bath-room door —
　　"Now get you gone!" quoth she.

FITTE THE FOURTH

Then from that tub and from that room
　　He gat with vast ado;

178

At every hop he gave a shake,
  And — how the water flew!

He paddled down the winding stairs
  And to the parlor hied,
Dispensing pools of foamy suds
  And slop on every side.

Upon the carpet then he rolled
  And brushed against the wall,
And, horror! whisked his lathery sides
  On overcoat and shawl.

Attracted by the dreadful din,
  His mistress came below —
Who, who can speak her wonderment—
  Who, who can paint her woe!

Great smears of soap were here and
    there —
  Her startled vision met
With blobs of lather everywhere,
  And everything was wet!

Then Mrs. Taylor gave a shriek
    Like one about to die:
"Get out — get out, and don't you dare
    Come in till you are dry!"

With that she opened wide the door
    And waved the critter through;
Out in the circumambient air
    With grateful yelps he flew.

FITTE THE FIFTH

He whisked into the dusty street
    And to the Waller lot,
Where bonnie Annie Evans played
    With charming Sissy Knott.

And with those pretty little dears
    He mixed himself all up —
Oh, fie upon such boisterous play —
    Fie, fie, you naughty pup!

Woe, woe on Annie's India mull,
    And Sissy's blue percale!
One got that pup's belathered flanks,
    And one his soapy tail!

Forth to the rescue of those maids
   Rushed gallant Willie Clow;
His panties they were white and clean—
   Where are those panties now?

Where is the nicely laundered shirt
   That Kendall Evans wore,
And Robbie James' tricot coat
   All buttoned up before?

The leaven, which, as we are told,
   Leavens a monstrous lump,
Hath far less reaching qualities
   Than a wet pup on the jump.

This way and that he swung and swayed,
   He gambolled far and near,
And everywhere he thrust himself
   He left a soapy smear.

FITTE THE SIXTH

That noon a dozen little dears
   Were spanked and put to bed
With naught to stay their appetites
   But cheerless crusts of bread.

That noon a dozen hired girls
    Washed out each gown and shirt
Which that exuberant Taylor pup
    Had frescoed o'er with dirt.

That whole day long the Aprile sun
    Smiled sweetly from above
On clotheslines flaunting to the breeze
    The emblems mothers love.

That whole day long the Taylor pup
    This way and that did hie
Upon his mad, erratic course,
    Intent on getting dry.

That night when Mr. Taylor came
    His vesper meal to eat,
He uttered things my pious pen
    Would liefer not repeat.

Yet still that noble Taylor pup
    Survives to romp and bark
And stumble over folks and things
    In fair Buena Park.

Good sooth, I wot he should be called
  Buena's favorite son
Who 's sired of such a noble sire
  And dammed by every one!

AFTER READING TROLLOPE'S HIS-
TORY OF FLORENCE

MY books are on their shelves again
And clouds lie low with mist and rain.
Afar the Arno murmurs low
The tale of fields of melting snow.
List to the bells of times agone
The while I wait me for the dawn.

Beneath great Giotto's Campanile
The gray ghosts throng; their whispers steal
From poets' bosoms long since dust;
They ask me now to go.   I trust
Their fleeter footsteps where again
They come at night and live as men.

The rain falls on Ghiberti's gates;
The big drops hang on purple dates;

And yet beneath the ilex-shades —
Dear trysting-place for boys and maids —
There comes a form from days of old,
With Beatrice's hair of gold.

The breath of lands or lilied streams
Floats through the fabric of my dreams;
And yonder from the hills of song,
Where psalmists brood and prophets throng,
The lone, majestic Dante leads
His love across the blooming meads.

Along the almond walks I tread
And greet the figures of the dead.
Mirandula walks here with him
Who lived with gods and seraphim;
Yet where Colonna's fair feet go
There passes Michael Angelo.

In Rome or Florence, still with her
Stands lone and grand her worshipper.
In Leonardo's brain there move
Christ and the children of His love;
And Raphael is touching now,
For the last time, an angel's brow.

Angelico is praying yet
Where lives no pang of man's regret,
And, mixing tears and prayers within
His palette's wealth, absolved from sin,
He dips his brush in hues divine;
San Marco's angel faces shine.

Within Lorenzo's garden green,
Where olives hide their boughs between,
The lovers, as they read betimes
Their love within Petrarca's lines,
Stand near the marbles found at Rome,
Lost shades that search in vain for home.

They pace the paths along the stream,
Dark Vallombrosa in their dream.
They sing, amidst the rain-drenched pines,
Of Tuscan gold that ruddier shines
Behind a saint's auroral face
That shows e'en yet the master's trace.

But lo, within the walls of gray,
E're yet there falls a glint of day,
And far without, from hill to vale,
Where honey-hearted nightingale
Or meads of pale anemones
Make sweet the coming morning breeze —

I hear a voice, of prophet tone,
A voice of doom, like his alone
That once in Gadara was heard;
The old walls trembled — lo, the bird
Has ceased to sing, and yonder waits
Lorenzo at his palace gates.

Some Romola in passing by
Turns toward the ruler, and his sigh
Wanders amidst the myrtle bowers
Or o'er the city's mantled towers,
For she is Florence! "Wilt thou hear
San Marco's prophet? Doom is near."

"Her liberties," he cries, "restore!
This much for Florence — yea, and more
To men and God!" The days are gone;
And in an hour of perfect dawn
I stand beneath the cypress trees
That shiver still with words like these.

A LULLABY

THE stars are twinkling in the skies,
    The earth is lost in slumbers deep;
So hush, my sweet, and close thine eyes,
    And let me lull thy soul to sleep.
Compose thy dimpled hands to rest,
    And like a little birdling lie
Secure within thy cozy nest
Upon my loving mother breast,
    And slumber to my lullaby,
    So hushaby — O hushaby.

The moon is singing to a star
    The little song I sing to you;
The father sun has strayed afar,
    As baby's sire is straying too.
And so the loving mother moon
    Sings to the little star on high;

And as she sings, her gentle tune
Is borne to me, and thus I croon
    For thee, my sweet, that lullaby
    Of hushaby — O hushaby.

There is a little one asleep
    That does not hear his mother's song;
But angel watchers — as I weep —
    Surround his grave the night-tide long.
And as I sing, my sweet, to you,
    Oh, would the lullaby I sing —
The same sweet lullaby he knew
While slumb'ring on this bosom too —
    Were borne to him on angel's wing!
    So hushaby — O hushaby.

"THE OLD HOMESTEAD"

JEST as atween the awk'ard lines a hand
  we love has penn'd
  Appears a meanin' hid from other eyes,
So, in your simple, homespun art, old honest
      Yankee friend,
  A power o' tearful, sweet seggestion lies.
We see it all — the pictur' that our mem'ries
    hold so dear —
  The homestead in New England far away,
An' the vision is so nat'ral-like we almost
    seem to hear
  The voices that were heshed but yester-
    day.

Ah, who 'd ha' thought the music of that
    distant childhood time
  Would sleep through all the changeful,
    bitter years
To waken into melodies like Chris'mas bells
    a-chime
  An' to claim the ready tribute of our tears!

Why, the robins in the maples an' the black-
    birds round the pond,
  The crickets an' the locusts in the leaves,
The brook that chased the trout adown the
    hillside just beyond,
  An' the swallers in their nests beneath the
    eaves —
They all come troopin' back with you, dear
    Uncle Josh, to-day,
  An' they seem to sing with all the joy-
    ous zest
Of the days when we were Yankee boys
    an' Yankee girls at play,
  With nary thought of "livin' way out
    West"!

God bless ye, Denman Thomps'n, for the
    good y' do our hearts
  With this music an' these memories o'
    youth —
God bless ye for the faculty that tops all
    human arts,
  The good ol' Yankee faculty of Truth!

CHRISTMAS HYMN

SING, Christmas bells!
  Say to the earth this is the morn
Whereon our Saviour-King is born;
    Sing to all men — the bond, the free,
The rich, the poor, the high, the low —
    The little child that sports in glee —
The aged folk that tottering go —
        Proclaim the morn
        That Christ is born,
    That saveth them and saveth me!

        Sing, angel host!
Sing of the star that God has placed
Above the manger in the east;
    Sing of the glories of the night,
The virgin's sweet humility,
    The Babe with kingly robes bedight —

Sing to all men where'er they be
    This Christmas morn,
    For Christ is born,
  That saveth them and saveth me!

    Sing, sons of earth!
O ransomed seed of Adam, sing!
God liveth, and we have a King!
  The curse is gone, the bond are free —
By Bethlehem's star that brightly beamed,
  By all the heavenly signs that be,
We know that Israel is redeemed —
    That on this morn
    The Christ is born
  That saveth you and saveth me!

    Sing, O my heart!
Sing thou in rapture this dear morn
Whereon the blessed Prince is born!
  And as thy songs shall be of love,
So let my deeds be charity —
  By the dear Lord that reigns above,
By Him that died upon the tree,
    By this fair morn
    Whereon is born
  The Christ that saveth all and me!

A PARAPHRASE OF HEINE

(LYRIC INTERMEZZO)

THERE fell a star from realms above —
   A glittering, glorious star to see!
Methought it was the star of love,
   So sweetly it illumined me.

And from the apple branches fell
   Blossoms and leaves that time in June;
The wanton breezes wooed them well
   With soft caress and amorous tune.

The white swan proudly sailed along
   And vied her beauty with her note —
The river, jealous of her song,
   Threw up its arms to clasp her throat.

But now — oh, now the dream is past —
   The blossoms and the leaves are dead,
The swan's sweet song is hushed at last,
   And not a star burns overhead.

THE CONVALESCENT GRIPSTER

THE gods let slip that fiendish grip
  Upon me last week Sunday —
No fiercer storm than racked my form
    E'er swept the Bay of Fundy;
  But now, good-by
  To drugs, say I —
    Good-by to gnawing sorrow;
  I am up to-day,
  And, whoop, hooray!
    I 'm going out to-morrow!

What aches and pain in bones and brain
    I had I need not mention;
It seemed to me such pangs must be
    Old Satan's own invention;
  Albeit I
  Was sure I 'd die,
    The doctor reassured me —

And, true enough,
With his vile stuff,
  He ultimately cured me.

As there I lay in bed all day,
  How fair outside looked to me!
A smile so mild old Nature smiled
  It seemed to warm clean through me.
In chastened mood
The scene I viewed,
  Inventing, sadly solus,
Fantastic rhymes
Between the times
  I had to take a bolus.

Of quinine slugs and other drugs
  I guess I took a million —
Such drugs as serve to set each nerve
  To dancing a cotillon;
The doctors say
The only way
  To rout the grip instanter
Is to pour in
All kinds of sin —
  Similibus curantur!

'T was hard; and yet I 'll soon forget
    Those ills and cures distressing;
One's future lies 'neath gorgeous skies
    When one is convalescing!
  So now, good-by
  To drugs say I —
   Good-by, thou phantom Sorrow!
  I am up to-day,
  And, whoop, hooray!
   I 'm going out to-morrow.

THE SLEEPING CHILD

MY baby slept — how calm his rest,
  As o'er his handsome face a smile
  Like that of angel flitted, while
He lay so still upon my breast!

My baby slept — his baby head
  Lay all unkiss'd 'neath pall and shroud:
  I did not weep or cry aloud —
I only wished I, too, were dead!

My baby sleeps — a tiny mound,
  All covered by the little flowers,
  Woos me in all my waking hours,
Down in the quiet burying-ground.

And when I sleep I seem to be
  With baby in another land —
  I take his little baby hand —
He smiles and sings sweet songs to me.

Sleep on, O baby, while I keep
  My vigils till this day be passed!
  Then shall I, too, lie down at last,
And with my baby darling sleep.

THE TWO COFFINS

IN yonder old cathedral
Two lovely coffins lie;
In one, the head of the state lies dead,
And a singer sleeps hard by.

Once had that King great power
And proudly ruled the land —
His crown e'en now is on his brow
And his sword is in his hand.

How sweetly sleeps the singer
With calmly folded eyes,
And on the breast of the bard at rest
The harp that he sounded lies.

The castle walls are falling
And war distracts the land,
But the sword leaps not from that mil-
dewed spot
There in that dead king's hand.

But with every grace of nature
   There seems to float along —
To cheer again the hearts of men —
   The singer's deathless song.

CLARE MARKET

IN the market of Clare, so cheery the glare
  Of the shops and the booths of the trades-
    people there;
That I take a delight on a Saturday night
In walking that way and in viewing the
    sight.
For it 's here that one sees all the objects
    that please —
New patterns in silk and old patterns in
    cheese,
For the girls pretty toys, rude alarums for
    boys,
And baubles galore while discretion enjoys —
But here I forbear, for I really despair
Of naming the wealth of the market of Clare.

A rich man comes down from the elegant
    town
And looks at it all with an ominous frown;
He seems to despise the grandiloquent cries

Of the vender proclaiming his puddings and
    pies;
And sniffing he goes through the lanes that
    disclose
Much cause for disgust to his sensitive nose;
And free of the crowd, he admits he is proud
That elsewhere in London this thing's not
    allowed;
He has seen nothing there but filth every-
    where,
And he 's glad to get out of the market of
    Clare.

But the child that has come from the gloom
    of the slum
Is charmed by the magic of dazzle and hum;
He feasts his big eyes on the cakes and the
    pies,
And they seem to grow green and protrude
    with surprise
At the goodies they vend and the toys with-
    out end —
And it 's oh! if he had but a penny to spend!
But alas, he must gaze in a hopeless amaze
At treasures that glitter and torches that
    blaze —

What sense of despair in this world can
    compare
With that of the waif in the market of Clare ?

So, on Saturday night, when my custom in-
    vites
A stroll in old London for curious sights,
I am likely to stray by a devious way
Where goodies are spread in a motley array,
The things which some eyes would appear
    to despise
Impress me as pathos in homely disguise,
And my battered waif-friend shall have pen-
    nies to spend,
So long as I 've got 'em (or chums that will
    lend);
And the urchin shall share in my joy and
    declare
That there 's beauty and good in the market
    of Clare.

A DREAM OF SPRINGTIME

I 'M weary of this weather and I hanker
   for the ways
Which people read of in the psalms and
   preachers paraphrase —
The grassy fields, the leafy woods, the
   banks where I can lie
And listen to the music of the brook that
   flutters by,
Or, by the pond out yonder, hear the red-
   wing blackbird's call
Where he makes believe he has a nest, but
   has n't one at all;
And by my side should be a friend — a
   trusty, genial friend,
With plenteous store of tales galore and
   natural leaf to lend;
Oh, how I pine and hanker for the gracious
   boon of spring —
For *then* I 'm going a-fishing with John
   Lyle King!

How like to pigmies will appear creation, as
    we float
Upon the bosom of the tide in a three-by-
    thirteen boat —
Forgotten all vexations and all vanities shall
    be,
As we cast our cares to windward and our
    anchor to the lee;
Anon the minnow-bucket will emit batrach-
    ian sobs,
And the devil's darning-needles shall come
    wooing of our bobs;
The sun shall kiss our noses and the breezes
    toss our hair
(This latter metaphoric — we 've no fimbriæ
    to spare!);
And I — transported by the bliss — shan't
    do a plaguey thing
But cut the bait and string the fish for John
    Lyle King!

Or, if I angle, it will be for bullheads and
    the like,
While he shall fish for gamey bass, for
    pickerel, and for pike;

I really do not care a rap for all the fish that
    swim —
But it 's worth the wealth of Indies just to
    be along with him
In grassy fields, in leafy woods, beside the
    water-brooks,
And hear him tell of things he 's seen or
    read of in his books —
To hear the sweet philosophy that trickles
    in and out
The while he is discoursing of the things
    we talk about;
A fountain-head refreshing — a clear, peren-
    nial spring
Is the genial conversation of John Lyle King!

Should varying winds or shifting tides re-
    dound to our despite —
In other words, should we return all boot-
    less home at night,
I 'd back him up in anything he had a mind
    to say
Of mighty bass he 'd left behind or lost upon
    the way;
I 'd nod assent to every yarn involving pis-
    cine game —

I 'd cross my heart and make my affidavit
    to the same;
For what is friendship but a scheme to help
    a fellow out —
And what a paltry fish or two to make such
    bones about!
Nay, Sentiment a mantle of sweet charity
    would fling
O'er perjuries committed for John Lyle King.

At night, when as the camp-fire cast a ruddy,
    genial flame,
He 'd bring his tuneful fiddle out and play
    upon the same;
No diabolic engine this — no instrument of
    sin —
No relative at all to that lewd toy, the violin!
But a godly hoosier fiddle — a quaint archaic
    thing
Full of all the proper melodies our grandmas
    used to sing;
With " Bonnie Doon," and " Nellie Gray,"
    and " Sitting on the Stile,"
" The Heart Bowed Down," the " White
    Cockade," and "Charming Annie Lisle "

SONGS AND OTHER VERSE

Our hearts would echo and the sombre
    empyrean ring
Beneath the wizard sorcery of John Lyle
    King.

The subsequent proceedings should interest
    me no more —
Wrapped in a woolen blanket should I
    calmly dream and snore;
The finny game that swims by day is my
    supreme delight —
And *not* the scaly game that flies in dark-
    ness of the night!
Let those who are so minded pursue this
    latter game
But not repine if they should lose a boodle
    in the same;
For an example to you all one paragon should
    serve —
He towers a very monument to valor and to
    nerve;
No bob-tail flush, no nine-spot high, no
    measly pair can wring
A groan of desperation from John Lyle King!

A truce to badinage — I hope far distant is
    the day

When from these scenes terrestrial our
    friend shall pass away!
We like to hear his cheery voice uplifted in
    the land,
To see his calm, benignant face, to grasp his
    honest hand;
We like him for his learning, his sincerity,
    his truth,
His gallantry to woman and his kindliness
    to youth,
For the lenience of his nature, for the vigor
    of his mind,
For the fulness of that charity he bears to
    all mankind —
That's why we folks who know him best
    so reverently cling
(And that is why I pen these lines) to John
    Lyle King.

And now adieu, a fond adieu to thee, O muse
    of rhyme —
I do remand thee to the shades until that
    happier time
When fields are green, and posies gay are
    budding everywhere,

And there 's a smell of clover bloom upon
    the vernal air;
When by the pond out yonder the redwing
    blackbird calls,
And distant hills are wed to Spring in veils
    of water-falls;
When from his aqueous element the fam-
    ished pickerel springs
Two hundred feet into the air for butterflies
    and things —
Then come again, O gracious muse, and
    teach me how to sing
The glory of a fishing cruise with John Lyle
    King!

UHLAND'S WHITE STAG.

INTO the woods three huntsmen came,
Seeking the white stag for their game.

They laid them under a green fir-tree
And slept, and dreamed strange things to
  see.

(FIRST HUNTSMAN)

I dreamt I was beating the leafy brush,
When out popped the noble stag — hush,
  hush!

(SECOND HUNTSMAN)

As ahead of the clamorous pack he sprang,
I pelted him hard in the hide — piff, bang!

212

(THIRD HUNTSMAN)

And as that stag lay dead I blew
On my horn a lusty tir-ril-la-loo!

So speak the three as there they lay
When lo! the white stag sped that way,

Frisked his heels at those huntsmen three,
Then leagues o'er hill and dale was he —
Hush, hush!   Piff, bang!   Tir-ril-la-loo!

HOW SALTY WIN OUT

USED to think that luck wuz luck and
  nuthin' else but luck —
It made no diff'rence how or when or where
  or why it struck;
But sev'ral years ago I changt my mind, an'
  now proclaim
That luck 's a kind uv science — same as any
  other game;
It happened out in Denver in the spring uv
  '80 when
Salty teched a humpback an' win out ten.

Salty wuz a printer in the good ol' Tribune
  days,
An', natural-like, he fell into the good ol'
  Tribune ways;

So, every Sunday evenin' he would sit into
    the game
Which in this crowd uv thoroughbreds I
    think I need not name;
An' there he 'd sit until he rose, an', when
    he rose, he wore
Invariably less wealth about his person than
    before.

But once there came a powerful change; one
    sollum Sunday night
Occurred the tidal wave that put ol' Salty
    out o' sight.
He win on deuce an' ace an' Jack — he win
    on king an' queen —
Clif Bell allowed the like uv how he win wuz
    never seen.
An' how he done it wuz revealed to all us
    fellers when
He said he teched a humpback to win out
    ten.

There must be somethin' in it, for he never
    win afore,
An' when he told the crowd about the
    humpback, how they swore!

For every sport allows it is a losin' game to
    luck
Agin the science uv a man who 's teched a
    hump f'r luck;
And there is no denyin' luck wuz nowhere
    in it when
Salty teched a humpback an' win out ten.

I 've had queer dreams an' seen queer things,
    an' allus tried to do
The thing that luck apparently intended f'r
    me to;
Cats, funerils, cripples, beggers have I treat-
    ed with regard,
An' charity subscriptions have hit me pow-
    erful hard;
But what 's the use uv talkin'? I say, an'
    say again:
You 've got to tech a humpback to win out
    ten!

So, though I used to think that luck wuz
    lucky, I 'll allow
That luck, for luck, agin a hump aint no-
    where in it now!

An' though I can't explain the whys an'
    wherefores, I maintain
There must be somethin' in it when the tip's
    so straight an' plain;
For I wuz there an' seen it, an' got full with
    Salty when
Salty teched a humpback an' win out ten!